THE SILVER BRANCH

THE SILVER BRANCH

A COLLECTION
OF THE BEST OLD IRISH LYRICS,
VARIOUSLY TRANSLATED

CHOSEN BY SEÁN O'FAOLÁIN

I bring you a branch of Evin's apple tree,
With silver twigs and crystal buds and blossoms . . .

Granger Index Reprint Series

 BOOKS FOR LIBRARIES PRESS
FREEPORT, NEW YORK

LIBRARY OF CONGRESS CATALOG CARD NUMBER:

68-58822

MANUFACTURED
BY
HALLMARK LITHOGRAPHERS, INC.
IN THE U.S.A.

ACKNOWLEDGMENTS

HERE and there, as the notes admit, I have shortened a longish poem, either as a concession to modern taste, or because the omitted parts are obscure. A more purely popular anthology could be made by a more severe "cutting," or by a more modern adaptation. But what little I have done in that way I have done almost with a feeling of being impertinent, and would not like to do more. In the notes, also, I give full acknowledgment of all the sources, but a general acknowledgment is needed to thank, on behalf of everybody, the scholars who first unearthed and pored over the manuscripts; were it not for their devotion and learning we should have lost an infinite pleasure. My own versions are reshapings based on a good knowledge of modern Irish, and some knowledge of Old Irish. Scholars find these reshapings by literary men something of an annoyance, and they have all my sympathy. I can only hope they will be appeased by the acknowledgment given in the notes, in each case, to the original, and, perhaps, only true "translators."

I wish, in particular, for permission to quote poems from books edited or published by them, to thank the following: Messrs. Williams & Norgate, Ltd., London (poems from *Silva Gaedelica,* edited by Standish O'Grady, London, 1892); The Irish Texts Society, London (poems from *The Adventures of Suibhne Geilt,* edited by James G. O'Keeffe, London, 1913); Charles Scribner, New York, and Ernest Benn, Ltd., London (poems from *Bards of Gael and Gall,* edited by George Sigerson, New York, 1907); The Henry Bradshaw Society, Magdalen College, Oxford (poems from

[5]

The Martyrology of Oengus, edited by Whitley Stokes, 1905); George G. Harrap & Co., Ltd., and Author ("May Day," by T. W. Rolleston, from *The High Deeds of Finn*); Constable & Co., Ltd. (poem from *Ancient Irish Poetry,* by Kuno Meyer); and to Dr. Osborn Bergin, Dr. Robin Flower, and Frank O'Connor for the translations over their names.

S. O'F.

CONTENTS

[7]

PART IV: EARLY COURT VERSE

Introduction

I

THESE poems I have winnowed carefully from all that, so far as I know, has been published over the last seventy-five years in the way of scholarly editions of Irish verse. It is, I think, a representative collection, for I made it for my own pleasure when I had the run of the Widener Library, at Harvard, and there was not a single book remotely connected with Irish scholarship on the shelves that I did not probe for good lyrics. At the time what I really wanted was the originals, not translations, for unhappily no collection of Irish verse, in the original Irish, had, at that date, ever been published. Having collected the texts I gathered the translations, mostly by the original editors (all of them men familiar with Old Irish): they are as near, in spirit or line, to the originals as I could find or dared, myself, try to make them. There is, I believe, nothing "romantic" or in the least "pseudo" about this book.

The lyrics are self-contained and need no explaining or praising. They are all anonymous, or ascribed to somebody like Oisin, or Columcille, who never wrote them. But they are so objective, and so dramatically impersonal, that we never feel anything of the vulgar modern desire to know about the author. Characteristically medieval, they do not exploit the ego; there is no exhibitionism; the lovely thing is made for its own sake, and may now and for ever be disliked or be loved for its own sake. A glance at the section which I have named The Heroic Tradition will note how utterly the poet has obliterated himself in order to speak as his subject, even though the persistent love of the Irishman for dramatic form has thrown almost every single poem into the (here impersonal-dramatic) first person. And even in a rare poem like "At Saint Patrick's Purgatory," which seems to be a purely personal, or individualistic, outburst of emotion, one cannot be sure that the man is not speaking in type, rather than for himself alone. From the danger of insincerity that might, elsewhere, follow on that convention, or racial tendency, these dramatic lyrics are secured by the hard objectivity of mind most evident in the nature verse. It is at best a lovely combination of personality and impersonality. Those who would like to make a comparison, in this regard, might like to read *Studies in Early Celtic Nature Poetry* by Kenneth Jackson (Cambridge University Press) where the Welsh and Irish poems are put side by side.

As to the artistry of these poets, one thing must be admitted—they rarely have any sense of total form; too often the poet delights in detail to an extravagant degree, and he will go on, and on, long after he should have stopped. This is not to apply modern ideas to an ancient form—the poet simply does not, in many cases, achieve any effect. Were it not for that, my collection would have been much larger. In the section called The Church will be found a pleasant little poem which I have entitled "The Desire for Hermitage"; the original form is more than twice as long and its prolixity spoils it. This is one of the few poems where I have dared to save the poet from himself. It may be added, however, that the old scribes quite evidently had no scruples about ruining good things in the opposite way—and may have done so with these verses. Such faults are frequent in all medieval art, where the artist is, apparently, never wholly conscious of his own purpose.

The originals are of a complexity of quatrain-form quite impossible to reproduce. Modern Irish poets like Mr. Austin Clarke or Mr. F. R. Higgins have, in a mild way, reproduced a little of their internal vowel and consonantal assonances, but they do not, wisely, try to repeat all the devices of the older craftsmen whose ingenuities are so numerous and so subtle as to escape, or even, when observed, to annoy, the untrained ear. But leaving out, altogether, the passage of time, and the deafening effect of over-familiarity with modern technique, we must recall that these poets underwent in the Bardic Schools a technical training that lasted anything from five to fifteen years. It is impossible, now, to say anything much to the point about the merits of the system ; the technical treatises which remain seem to us either pedantic, crazy, thorough, or murderous to inspiration, according to personal taste and prejudice.

Possibly the word "inspiration" would have meant little to these grammarians of poetry—in our sense at any rate. And, most troublesome of all, it must also be remembered that these fifty-odd poems are but a tiny proportion of masses of technically admirable, but otherwise inconceivably dull, dish-waterish drivel such as can have pleased no one but the pedants of any conceivable æsthetic. If one can conceive of a conventional training that would allow a man to write arid drivel today, and a lyric like "Summer Has Come" or "The Monk and His Cat" tomorrow, then one may also believe that the poems here collected were written within those "schools of poetry." I do not believe it. Though my disbelief is weakened by remembering that, far later, in

[11]

the seventeenth and eighteenth centuries, where we have collections by known individuals, like Aodhagáin O'Rathaille, or, later still, Piaras MacGhearailt, we find men writing drivel by the yard, and, embedded in that conventional stuff, lovely, fiery, personal poetry—not much, perhaps three poems in a heavy volume of O'Rathaille's, perhaps but one in MacGhearailt, but one good poem is enough to puzzle us in such company. That elaborate schooling, indeed, may have been merely a symptom, not a cause, of dullness; the deeper cause may lie in the traditionalism of a whole racial mind. But that is a matter that would take us far from poetry into the effective causes dear to the heart of the sociologist. All that is certain is that these poems, in this small gathering, came in single spies, and that the mass of the work of the schools of poetry, as it remains, is dull stuff.

Apart from the Bardic Schools the one other great cultural body in this Ireland was the Irish Church; and it will be noticed that the Irish Church contributes directly the least part of this anthology. A student of that Church could write a very sardonic account of its conventions. He would set it off by a very enthusiastic account of its evangelical work; but if he were tempted, as so many have been, to go further and speak of the culture it spread through Europe, he would, also, have to say, in all honesty, that literature was not part of that culture. In elaborate goldwork, in incomparable coloured designs for books, in fine, masculine, simple architecture, the Irish Church can show many examples of creative power; but for literature—No! Its hagiology is without merit. It did not found a school of history. In philosophy the list is, with one exception (a dishonourable one to the thinking of the Church), a blank. Perhaps one does not expect poetry from a Church? But there are always the great medieval hymns—always names like Jacopone da Todi—to chide the Irish monks. It does not help to say that since all these lyrics are anonymous it might be that a love-snatch, here as elsewhere, was written in a bothy or a cell—there is, in the second section, an excellent descriptive poem, "The Hermit and the King," possibly by a monk, and in the first see "The Desire for Hermitage." The fact remains that the Church has left us no mass of real literature connected with its life.

As to the final section, it is brief, mainly because the ulterior date I have chosen is around 1400. By shifting the date forward it could be lengthened to fill a volume, and always, then, there would be at least a line to save a poem from emptiness; but it would definitely represent the beginning of the end. For by then poetry had become professional in subject, treatment, and author. The Church is asleep; the schools alone go on. Here could go a variety of formal verse, eulogies, elegies, poems on place-names, political verse, all of it cursed by pedantry, and preserved only by unthinking traditionalism. It would be the counterpart of the folly of the Irish chiefs, who, from the settling-down of the Normans in Ireland to the settling-down of the Tudors in England, had about two hundred years in which to do what they liked with their country, and did nothing with it. It was in a Norman-Irish convention that the best, perhaps the only, poetry was written in that time, a fashioned love-poetry in the style of, for example, Richard Burke's lines (so well translated by Robin Flower):

> We will not die, these lovers say,
> For any eyes but eyes of blue;
> No hair shall win our hearts away
> But hair of golden hue.

It is not with me as with those,
And yet, a wiser song I sing,
Whom a love-lighted eye can please
Black as the raven's wing.

I ask no roses in her face,
No golden shimmer in her hair;
A pallid cheek for me has grace,
And jet-black locks are fair.

Dark was the mother of that maid
Who brought proud Ilion to its fall;
Yet shining locks of golden braid
Had Helen fair and tall.

Which was the lovelier of the two—
Red-lipped, sweet-voiced, that winsome pair—
There was no man on earth that knew;
The dark one or the fair.

That was in a convention. So, no doubt, is this earlier lyric verse. Neither is ossified like the earlier school, or Bardic poetry, or the later court poetry. Personality may be hidden in Richard Burke's lines, as it is fitting it should; and in these lyrics, as the authors chose. Beside them, many— and after them nearly all—do not so much hide their personalities as get along without any. It is not that the schools and the churchmen, that is to say, wrote in a convention— they simply did not write *because* of the convention.

II

Because, however, of this other accepted and controlled (not controlling) convention of our lyric poets, the convention of impersonality, we are separated for ever from their lives and minds. Each had, no doubt, a private life, but we shall never know it. One reads these verses today, a thousand years after they were written, and even when one lights on a source—such as the sayings of the philosophers at Alexander's tomb (for a poem which I do not think it right to give); or the epic stories, for the poems in the section, The Heroic Tradition; or a Biblical phrase, for a religious poem; or a bit of folklore, for a poem like "The Vision of Ita"— it leaves everything just as before. It is still an unclaimed poem by a medieval Irishman, long since clay. Only here and there can we see life and the re-creating imagination meet, and feel that we have seen beauty born.

These rare, informative poems are for the most part poems of friendship, and nature, and "history," and we do well to think of these three subjects as compensations in the poet's simple life. Poems on these subjects are not rare in the medieval literature of Europe, and no doubt for that life also were compensations hardly earned.

Where they occur they usually have a flavour strange to all other poetry, a flavour suggestive of a world that is at once sturdy and gentle, recalling to our minds, as individualistic poetry never does, the homeliness and stability of "average" life. The same homely flavour hangs over Irish poems on the same themes; they make us feel, as nothing else in them does, part of themselves.

Nowhere else do we get such intimate detail; they are so full of it that they might appear to be written to a theory; indeed, if their touch was not so intimate we might be less troubled by the mystery of its anonymity. So when, as in the set of poems in the *Guesting of Athirne,* we are told,

In the dark seasons of deep winter,
heavy seas are lifted up,
Along the side of the world's region . . .
Hounds wax insolent from cracking bones;
the iron vessel is put upon the fire
throughout the dark, black day . . .

we must feel in those last three lines as near to the elbow of
the writer as when we overhear the marginalia of the scribes.
There one will whisper of a stain on his vellum—*Blood
from the finger of Melaghlin;* or another, having copied out
some pathetic story, write in the margin, *'Tis sad, O little
book;* or a third, caught gazing vacantly out of the window.
The cat has gone astray; the robin is all red; I am alone.

The poems of friendship, in particular, have this same
quality of intimacy and something in addition: though they
do not describe or comment on the world of the hearth, perhaps never mention the word home, they are an integral part
of the life of the home and to read them is to feel that one
has, in turn, been assimilated for a moment by part of the
medieval world.

> Play was each, pleasure each,
> Till Ferdiad faced the beach;
> One had been our student life,
> One in strife of school our place,
> One our gentle teacher's grace
>   Loved o'er all and each. . . .

> Play was each, pleasure each,
> Till Ferdiad faced the beach;
> Dear that pillar of pure gold
> Who fell cold beside the ford.

Hosts of heroes felt his sword
First in battle's breach. . . .

Play was each, pleasure each,
Till Ferdiad faced the beach;
Loved Ferdiad, dear to me:
I shall dree his death for aye—
Yesterday a Mountain he,
A Shade today.

Reading such verse we forget the crazy traditions (of the
Bardic Schools) that gave it suck. We do, however, realize
equally that it was not written in an individualistic mood,
that it owes a great deal to an entirely traditional manner
of life and thought.

As to the use of "history" as a theme, there exists an il-
luminating catalogue of the reading-material of medieval
Ireland which tells us what traditional material was to hand
when the poet needed to throw his ideas into a dramatic
form without disclosing fully his own personal life.[1]

There is here the usual list of Raids, Burnings, Wooings,
Wars, Visions, Massacres, and so forth, and here and there
one sees the possible source of one of our unfathered, un-
christened, unacknowledged poems. The poem just quoted
is based on an episode in the major epic of the Bull of
Cooley; there is also the story of Deirdre, and Dermot, and
Finn, whose colour and fragrance in the memory of medieval Ireland issued, as the endless genealogies and their like
could not, in the shape of poems of deep feeling. That we
have and may enjoy verse written about those old traditional stories tells us much. Reading his verses we know

[1] *Essai d'un Catalogue: D'Arbois de Jubainville*, Paris, 1883, pp. 260 ff.

that the poet's mind was filled with the fumes of their wine and that to the chimeras of those immemorial tales he felt no such opposition as overcame him in the presence of the learned fictions of the scholars' verses. Those tales were surely to him what the folk-tradition is to us, the simple communal art of the people, disorganized, helter-skelter, demanding no individual loyalty to a literary form, seeking to impose no literary type, having about them nothing of a hard and fast tradition or a circumscribing habit. Those stories, obviously prepared for the largest audiences, were, if they actually came from the schools, the one justification for those schools. There is little formalism about them, however: they are frequently little more than dissolving memories, in which new inventions mingle with old, contradicting one another frequently just as do the folk tales of the present day. (There is no one coherent epic in Irish: the *Tain,* or *The Driving of the Bull of Cooley,* is disorganized as it stands—the key episode of the swoon of the Ultonians, for example, is left unexplained, and one must go to another tale for the solution—and it should be a bold scholar who would say that it was ever otherwise. So, too, Fionn and Ossian are preserved under such a multitude of forms that there are widely differing accounts of Fionn's birth, death, and personal character, while it is the amusement of scholars to invent for him a workable chronology.)

How relieved our poets must have been to find it so—nothing but pure air around the figures of Deirdre, the Children of Lir, the love of Diarmuid for Grainne, the characters of Fionn and Ossian. These were the free gift of the most vital of his kin who had gone before him, and in calling on them to be his joy and his sorrow for the space of the composition of a poem he need have felt himself under no obligation to bards or genealogists. With his verse before us, and a knowledge of his day, we need feel no compunction in saying that, within the limits of an accepted story, he treated this material according to his own will only, just as in our day Yeats or A. E. or Austin Clarke —as unaware as he was, for once, free of presanctified taboos —have used for their own ends the inspiration of the very same tales.

It is an amusing warning to those who would demur at this to note how, when he did so, his more formal contemporaries attempted to drag him into their circle once more. We come repeatedly on little verses on Nature, put into the mouths of characters from the tales—verses as simple as a bird's flight. They are frequently found embedded in prose intended to explain their composition to those conventional minds to whom it was unthinkable that the traditional introduction might be dispensed with: *"place, person, time, and occasion"*—for it was a convention of the formal that nothing could exist without stating each of them clearly. So scholarly commentators from the schools coming on these flowerlike poems proceeded to bury them in the usual incredible history, brazenly inventing "place, person, time, and occasion," thence proceeding happily to some equally futile task.[1] (See pages 56 and 90.)

We need not imitate the Bardic scholars. They had not observed what (as I have remarked already) even a cursory glance through an anthology of these lyrics will reveal —that there is scarcely an Irish poem of the period (I do not know more than a dozen) which is not written in the first person. Dramatic form is characteristic of Irish literature as a whole, but for the reason that one does not expect

---

[1] V. *Thes. Pal.* II, 323. Here four alternative explanations are given for a simple hymn, no one being a whit more likely than the other. Kuno Meyer explains the process in *Rev. Celt.* XI, 127.

to find it so consistently in lyric poetry one feels that it is a mode adopted after intimate and interested communication with the drama of the heroic sagas. Had those later glossators felt the drama of the communal literature as appreciatively as those previous poets felt it, they would not have thought to complicate simplicity with their irrelevant glosses; all the simplification needed of them and us is some recognition of the qualities of their national genius. Synge, in making of his Deirdre something of a player-queen, aware of the drama of her own fate, sensed accurately this self-consciousness of his race: "There will be a story told of a ruined city and a raving king and a woman will be young for ever . . . a thing will be a joy and triumph to the ends of life and time." In the remarkable eighth-century poem called "The Tryst with Death," the dying Fian says with an identical vainglory: "Someone will at all times remember (my) lay—my discourse with thee shall not be unrenowned if thou but consider my request of thee."

It was, indeed, a complication of simplicity to annotate these personal poems as the scribes did with their "person, place, time, and occasion." It was a decline of tradition—or a new, and base, tradition fouling the old one. Yeats tells how he admired the breadth and stability of the old poetry, and longed to fashion a poetry of "unpremeditated joyous imagery" like those statues of Mausolus and Artemisia in the British Museum, although, being a man of modern times, he could not but "model his own image on Pallas Athena's buckler." What he goes on to say is true of those personal poets: " 'Elaborate modern psychology sounds egotistical,' I thought, 'when it speaks in the first person, but not those simple emotions which resemble the more, the more powerful they are, everybody's emotion, and I was soon to write many poems where an always personal emotion was woven into a general pattern of myth and symbol.'" These old lyrists of ours often did exactly that—nearly always did that. Irish balladists keep on doing it. It is racial. A personal emotion woven into a "general pattern"—it is the note of Irish literature in every age. These old Irish lyrics gain all their power, and much of their charm, from that mingling of personal and general, individual and racial, the moment of the man compressing the time of man into a verse.

Nature, it would seem, these lyrists discovered for themselves. With one or two exceptions only, in thousands upon thousands of lines of prose saga-material, natural description does not occur in Irish literature outside these lyrics. Such a book as *The Old Men's Gossip* (*Agallamh na Senorach*), which is a prose and verse hotch-potch of Ossianic material, represents what was available for an anthology covering the seven hundred years between the origin of the Fenian cycle and the date of the compilation of the miscellany in the fourteenth century, and here, wherever there is specific treatment of natural beauty, it occurs in verse only. Irish ornament makes next to no use of natural objects in its design—one finds mostly the trefoil and the lotus—and no one has yet suggested that the poet had any other models for his natural description but the original beauty around him. If it be really true that he discovered the beauty of Nature for himself it is his greatest triumph. His verse is no better and no worse for being the first poetry west of the Danube to treat of her as a friend, gentle and lovable, too beautiful to die [1]: it is no better for that, but it is a great

---

[1] Dauzat: *Le Sentiment de la Nature,* Paris, 1914, pp. 172 ff. He appears to draw largely on Victor de Laprade, *Le Sentiment de la Nature,* Paris, 1886.

personal triumph. It gauges his sensitiveness, his authentic genius, and it signs his nationality. Across the Irish Sea his Saxon contemporaries—beginning a little later—found in the storms that so delighted him, that so stirred his soul, for the most part nothing but the symbol of disintegration. If one quarrels with them at all, it is not because they did not find in it a symbol of human power, or of resurrection, or some more comforting idea than death and transience: one rather wonders at them for finding in the storm, let us say, not beauty but a symbol. M. Émile Pons pointed out a few years ago, in a paper on Old English verse, how indigenous is that English sentimental attitude to Nature. He is probably right. I believe that an examination of even Anglo-Irish verse would show how foreign to the native Irish genius such an attitude would be, and find in all Irish literature the same traditional objectivity of these Old Irish lyric poems on natural objects.

Image after image clinches in a line some aspect of the season in their poems on winter and summer. Who will not recognize winter itself in,

> A river is each furrow on the slope,

or summer in,

> The sail gathers, perfect peace!

or who needs to be told what season this is:—

> Blades of corn lie around cornfields
> over the region of the brown world,

or fail to feel the spring in each line of:—

> The cold will spring up in one's face:
> the ducks of the pool have raised a cry,

from wildernesses wolf-packs scent
the early rise of morning-time.

I have said that we know nothing about these poets, whether
they were men or women, young or old—and yet I think
one can tell safely that they were, whatever they professed
to be, pure pagans. There is not the slightest trace of even
a pantheistic belief in their Nature verse; Nature *was,* and
nothing more; as in this random, and isolated, quatrain:

> Cold the night in Moin Moir,
> a powerful rainstorm pours down;
> a wild tune—at which the clear wind laughs—
> is wailing over the shelter of the woods.

One can believe that the poet turned with an equal vitality
to almost everything that in his daily life he had to meet.
That objectivity recompenses us for the mystery of his name.
If we but let a little freedom to our sympathies we can feel
back at his side in an instant, unsundered by strangeness
in his beliefs or ours, at one with his delight, indifferent
to his mask.

When he says, with the air of a man looking over a half-
door, in another isolated scrap:

> A little bird
> has let a piping from the tip
> of his shining yellow beak—
> the blackbird from the yellow-leaved tree
> has flung his whistle over Loch Laig,

(and that, by the way, is all there is of it), we can surely feel
the same physical delight, the same identical pleasure that
he felt, and nothing to mar that pleasure but the withdrawal

[23]

of our smile in thinking, with a melancholy that has nothing to do with the little poem, that bird, and tree, and whistle—and man—passed out of this world almost a thousand years ago.

That is as near to the poet as we ever come. He shares his subject and his emotion; in fact he transfers it; he keeps himself to himself apart from the moment of creation.

III

In such things, then, we get a half-glimpse of the authors of these lyrics, because it was with such things—Nature and dramatic character—that they saved their humanity from the inhumanity of the Church and the schools. Nature, and the old epic tales, and snatches of humble folk-life or folklore, were, then as today, the corrective of the artist for the over-organized, over-traditionalized state. The bards might be well paid, and these men not; they might pretend to play at voodoo, and impress the ignorant and the wealthy —especially the wealthy—and these men not; the monks might live in comfort of body and an easy mind, and these men not; but these had consolations that those had not. The same popular life, the same realistic literature, did, in later days, exactly the same duty for such men as Yeats. As these lyrists, his forebears, found delight in Maeve, the tall amazon of the epics, he, when she had declined in glory with the passage of time, found delight in hearing Biddy Early talking of her, in her latter-day role, as "the queen of all the western fairies."

But, perhaps, it is no matter to decide whether or not these lyrics came out of the schools or out of lonely lives. Irish literature is full of contradictions—like the Irish character. And it is merely one of many contradictions to find a beautiful verse buried in stupid prose, a delicate passage suddenly lighting up a banal tale. One reads the book called *The Old Men's Gossip* and is suddenly about to throw it aside when a charming lyric blossoms magically in the wilderness; one is dropping asleep over a succession of wearisome duels in the *Tain,* when the writing suddenly becomes, for a second, astonishingly graphic, to describe a cloven body being dragged Hector-like at the heels of a chariot—"at the rocky places it divides in two and at the smooth places it comes together again"; in the middle of that scarcely intelligible rhapsody "The Praise," or "Amra, of Columcille," one comes on four beautiful quatrains on winter, almost the sole recompense for the perusal of that ponderous eulogy; and conversely, when one is reading with pleasure, in the story of Deirdre or the Voyage of Bran, a kenning will remind one of some such Bardic imbecility as the adoption of that gasconade in grammar which, according to Zimmer, Virgilius Maro foisted on the gullible Irish schools.

One pleads for the idea of the individual Irish poet, as against the traditional, simply because the traditional poet was at all periods futile, because the individuality of poetry is for all periods, to some degree, a loyalty that no critic can reject, and because the very anonymity of these poets, in this collection, together with their excellence, seems to beg from us at least some sort of differentiation between the individual and the mass whose indifference has swallowed him for ever.

SEÁN O'FAOLÁIN

PART I

The Church

Starry Sky

O King of the starry sky,
lest Thou from me withdraw Thy light—
whether my house be dark or bright,
my door shall close on none tonight.

S. O'F.

The Vision of Ita

Saint Ita sees Christ come to her in a vision as a baby to be nursed:

It is Jesukin
who is nursed by me in my little hermitage:
though it be a cleric with treasures,
all is a lie save Jesukin.

The nursing I do in my house
is not the nursing of a base clown:
Jesus with the men of Heaven
under my heart every single night.

Young Jesukin, my eternal good!
to heed him is a cause of forgiveness,
the king who controls all things,
not to beseech Him will cause repentance.

It is Jesus, noble, angelic,
not an unlearned cleric,
who is fostered by me in my little hermitage,
Jesus the son of the Hebrew woman.

Sons of princes, sons of kings,
though they should come into my country,
I should not expect profit from them;
more likely, I think, from Jesukin.

Sing ye a chorus, O maidens,
to Him who has a right to your little tribute,
who sits in his place above,
though Jesukin is at my breast.

WHITLEY STOKES

The Heavenly Banquet

(Ascribed to Saint Bridget)

I would like to have the men of Heaven
in my own house;
with vats of good cheer
laid out for them.

I would like to have the three Marys,
their fame is so great.
I would like people
from every corner of Heaven.

I would like them to be cheerful
in their drinking.
I would like to have Jesus, too,
here amongst them.

I would like a great lake of beer
for the King of Kings.
I would like to be watching Heaven's family
drinking it through all eternity.

S. O'F.

[31]

Penitentes

I

"A very ancient old vellum book states that Munna the
son of Tulchain was in his habits and life like unto Job."

Mac Tulchain, by his own wish,
never touched his flesh;
in all the torments of the itch
he never stooped to scratch.

II

"He used also to lie the first night in the same grave with
every corpse that used to be buried in his church."

On hooks beneath his arm-pits
For Christ's blessing on his soul,
Fionnchu hung for seven years;
the earth never smirched his sole.

III

"Fer da Leithe was another name for this man, i.e., he
spent half his life in Scotland, and the other half in Erin."

And if I *have* a soldier's head,
I got it on the plains of Meath,
Or in that softer feather-bed,
A Scottish heath.

IV

"This is the Brendan who forsook patrimony, friends, and relations, and went on a pilgrimage over the Atlantic."

The most strenuous form of consecration
was chosen by Brendan, and by him alone;
according to synod and congregation,
he sat seven years on a whale's backbone.

S. O'F.

The Desire for Hermitage

Ah! To be all alone in a little cell
with nobody near me;
beloved that pilgrimage
before the last pilgrimage to Death.

To be cleansing my flesh with good habits,
trampling it down like a man;
to be weeping wearily,
paying for my passions.

A cold bed of fear—
the lying down of a doomed man;
a short sleep, waking to danger;
tears from early morning.

Dry bread portioned out
a good thing to hollow the face;
an end to gossip; no more fables;
the knees constantly bent.

That will be an end to evil
when I am alone
in a lovely little corner among tombs
far from the houses of the great.

Ah! To be all alone in a little cell,
to be alone, all alone,
alone as I came into the world—
and as I shall go from it.

S. O'F.

At Saint Patrick's Purgatory

Pity me on my pilgrimage to Loch Derg!
O King of the churches and the bells—
bewailing your sores and your wounds,
but not a tear can I squeeze from my eyes!

Not moisten an eye
after so much sin!
Pity me, O King! What shall I do
with a heart that seeks only its own ease?

Without sorrow or softening in my heart,
bewailing my faults without repenting them!
Patrick the high priest never thought
that he would reach God in this way.

O lone son of Calpurn—since I name him—
O Virgin Mary, how sad is my lot!—
he was never seen as long as he was in this life
without the track of tears from his eyes.

In a narrow, hard, stone-wall cell
I lie after all my sinful pride—
O woe, why cannot I weep a tear!—
and I buried alive in the grave.

On the day of Doom we shall weep heavily,
both clergy and laity;
the tear that is not dropped in time,
none heeds in the world beyond.

[35]

I shall have you go naked, go unfed,
body of mine, father of sin,
for if you are turned Hellwards
little shall I reck your agony tonight.

O only begotten Son by whom all men were made,
who shunned not the death by three wounds,
pity me on my pilgrimage to Loch Derg
and I with a heart not softer than a stone!

S. O'F.

PART II

The Woods, the Mountains, the Sea

The Open-Air Scriptorium

Over my head the forest wall
Rises; the ousel sings to me;
Above my booklet lined for words
The woodland birds shake out their glee.

There's the blithe cuckoo chanting clear
In mantle grey from bough to bough;
God keep me still! For here I write
His gospel bright in great woods now.

ROBIN FLOWER

The Monk and His Cat

Pangur Ban and I—
each at his own craft:
his mind is intent on mice,
and mine on my own trade.

Better than any fame I love ease
and deep study in my little book:
Pangur Ban bears me no envy;
he loves his own childish play.

When we are all alone in our house—
it is a tale I never weary of telling—
we each have—and what an endless sport it is!—
something against which we test our wits.

Now and again, after daring foray,
a mouse catches in his net—
meanwhile there falls into my net
some difficult rule of subtle sense.

He directs against the wall-boards
his eye, full of obscurity,
while I direct against the ramparts of knowledge
my bright, if ageing, eye.

He rejoices, swiftly racing,
until his sharp nails catch a mouse;
and if I have grasped a difficult, dear problem,
I too rejoice.

And though we are always so
neither hinders the other;
each loves his own craft
and pleases himself in his own way.

He is master of the trade
he follows every day:
so am I in mine,
when I put my finger on an answer.

S. O'F.

May Day

May day! delightful day!
Bright colours play the vale along.
Now wakes at morning's slender ray
Wild and gay the blackbird's song.

Now comes the bird of dusty hue,
The loud cuckoo, the summer-lover;
Branchy trees are thick with leaves;
The bitter, evil time is over.

Swift horses gather nigh
Where half dry the river goes;
Tufted heather clothes the height;
Weak and white the bogdown blows.

Corncrake sings from eve to morn,
Deep in corn a strenuous bard!
Sings the virgin waterfall, white and tall
Her one sweet word.

Loaded bees with puny power
Goodly flower-harvest win;
Cattle roam with muddy flanks;
Busy ants go out and in.

Through the wild harp of the wood
Making music roars the gale—
Now it settles without motion,
On the ocean sleeps the sail

Men grow mighty in the May,
Proud and gay the maidens grow;
Fair is every wooded height;
Fair and bright the plain below.

A bright shaft has smit the streams,
With gold gleams the water-flag;
Leaps the fish and on the hills
Ardor thrills the leaping stag.

Loudly carols the lark on high,
Small and shy his tireless lay,
Singing in wildest, merriest mood,
Delicate-hued, delightful May.

                                T. W. ROLLESTON

Summer Has Come

Summer has come, healthy and free,
whence the brown wood is aslope;
the slender nimble deer leap,
and the path of seals is smooth.

The cuckoo sings sweet music,
whence there is smooth restful sleep;
gentle birds leap upon the hill,
and swift grey stags.

Heat has laid hold of the rest of the deer—
the lovely cry of curly packs!
The white extent of the strand smiles;
There the swift sea falls.

A sound of playful breezes in the tops
of a black oakwood in Drum Daill,
The noble hornless herd runs,
to whom Cuan wood is a shelter.

Green bursts out on every herb,
the top of the green oakwood is bushy.
Summer has come, winter has gone;
twisted hollies wound the hound.

The blackbird sings a loud strain,
to him the live wood is a heritage,
the sad angry sea is fallen asleep,
the speckled salmon leaps.

The sun smiles over every land—
a parting for me from a brood of cares:
hounds bark, stags tryst,
ravens flourish. Summer is come!

KUNO MEYER

Autumn Song

A good stay-at-home season is Autumn; then there's work
    to be done by all:
Speckled fawns, where the branches make covert, range
    away undeterred;
And stags that were seen upon hillocks, now give heed to
    the call,
To the bellowing call of the hinds, and they draw back to
    the herd.

A good stay-at-home season is Autumn; the brown world's
    marked into fields;
The corn is up to its growth; the acorns teem in the wood;
By the side of the down-fallen fort even the thornbush yields
A crop, and there by the rath the hazelnuts drop from a
    load.

PADRAIC COLUM

Cellach's Poem to the Dawn

Cellach, a disciple of Ciaran of Clonmacnoise, was carried off into the woods by four recreants who had sworn to murder him. He begged for a night's respite and they put him into a hollow oak and sate at the entrance until the morning. Cellach slept not at all: even if he were to escape from the tree he could not walk far, for it was just after Lent and his body was weak from long fasting; so that when the dawn came he closed the entrance in terror of the light. But he feels that he must meet his judgment and flings open the door again. Just then the birds cry out in unison, the scaldcrow and the wren and all the waking birds—the kite of the yew tree of Cluain Eo, and the wolf of Druim-mac-Dair who had his haunt beneath the island banks. And he says:

Welcome, pale morning,
that cometh on the floor of my little cell,
welcome be the sender
of the everyoung victorious dawn.

Pale proud morning,
sister of the pure sun;
welcome be the pale morning,
lighting for me my little breviary.

It sees the guest of every house,
it lights every state and tribe;
welcome, O whitethroated dawn,
O golden-fair, fierce-blazing candle.

[47]

My little printspeckled book
tells me that my life has not been over-virtuous;
now must I fear Maelcróin
coming to strike me down at the end.

O scaldcrow, and O scaldcrow,
little greyhooded, beaked bird,
I see the intent of your desire;
you are no friend of Cellach's.

O raven, making croaking,
if you are hungry, O bird,
leave not this rath
until you have eaten your fill of flesh.

The kite of the yew tree of Cluain Eo
will share in the rough scramble;
he will carry off his fill of his grey talons,
loath to part with me.

The fox of the gloomy wood
will share readily the deathblow,
eating my flesh and blood
in cold, hidden places.

The wolf of the rath
East of Druim-mac-Dair,
will come at me
heading the handsome flock.

I saw a vision like that
this Wednesday past,
wild wolves dragging me in a pack
hither and thither in the red bracken.

O little wren, with the little tail,
pity the story's end you sing;
if you have come to betray me
and to shorten the days of my life.

S. O'F.

The Hermit and the King

Guaire:

Marbhan, O hermit,
why dost thou not sleep in a bed?
More often thou sleepest in the air
thy head stretched along a pine-root.

Marbhan:

I have a little hut in the wood
unknown to all save my Lord:
on this side an ash, on the other a hazel,
an old tree hangs over it.

It has two doorposts of heather to support it,
and a threshold of honeysuckle:
the wood about its narrow space
sheds mast for the fat swine.

The size of my hut is—small, but not too small,
many are its familiar paths:
a sweet strain falls from its gable—
she sings in her cloak of raven's colour.

The stags of Druim Rolach leap
into its stream, bordered by pure fields,
visible from there is red Roigne,
noble Mucraimi, and Maonmag.

The hiding foliage of a green yew tree
supports the sky:
fair spot! the wide greenery of an oak
stands against the bad weather.

A tree of apples, great its crop,
sheltering, widespread:
a pretty bush fistful with little hazelnuts
branching, green.

An excellent well, a fall of water,
noble to drink:
watercresses and yewberries grow there,
and flourishing ivy.

Tame swine hide around it,
goats and hogs,
wild pigs, grazing deer,
and a badger-warren.

A peaceful host, a whole flock of land-dwellers
visit my dwelling:
foxes come to ambush them—
is not that delightful?

Princely excellence comes to my house
in ready offering:
pure water, ever-flourishing bushes,
salmon, trout.

[51]

Rowanberry, black sloes,
dun blackthorns,
plenty of food, acorns, lean berries,
smooth flags.

A clutch of eggs, honey, sweet mast,
God has bestowed it all:
sweet apples, red cranberries,
heather berries.

Ale of herbs, a vessel of strawberries,
tasting well, coloured well,
haws, yewberries,
sloes, nuts.

A cup of hazelnut mead, bluebells,
quick rushes,
little dun oaks, thorny brier,
and good sweet-tangle.

If summer be gentle and its mantle coloured,
what delicious dainties—
pignuts, wild marjoram, green leeks,
green and pure.

The strains of the bright redbreasted little fellows
most dear to me:
the deep song of the thrush, the ever-fair cuckoos,
above my hut.

Swarms of bees, chafers, the little musicians of the world,
make gentle humming:
wild geese, woodcocks, near by Samhain,
announcing the dark torrent.

The able bird, the battling wren,
from the hazel branch,
beautiful hooded woodpeckers
in a great flock.

There come white birds, cranes, seagulls,
the cuckoo sings,
nor is his music sad; dun henbirds rise
out of the red heather.

The clamour of the heifers in the summer,
brightest season of all;
it is not bitter or hard going over the fertile plain,
delightful and smooth.

The wind cries against the woven wood;
A grey cloud passes;
river waterfalls; the cry of the swan;
delightful music.

The fairest of herds makes music for me,
and that without a foray,
I am thankful for what has been given me
by my fair Christ.

Without once in strife, without the din of fighting,
in my house,
grateful to the King who gives me every good thing
in my bothy.

Guaire:

I would give my glorious kingdom
with my share of Colman's heritage:
I would forfeit it to the hour of my death
to be in thy company, Marbhan.

S. O'F.

Summer Is Gone

I have but one story—
the stags are moaning,
the sky is snowing,
Summer is gone.

Quickly the low sun
goes drifting down
behind the rollers,
lifting and long.

The wild geese cry
down the storm;
the ferns have fallen,
russet and torn.

The wings of the birds
are clotted with ice.
I have but one story—
Summer is gone.

S. O'F.

A Cold Night

Mac Lesc (The Lazy Boy), son of Ladan, a fat loon who was of Finn's household, 'tis he that sang these quatrains below. It happened one night that he and Finn were separated from the war-band at Colt's standing-stone on Slieve Gullion when Finn sent him to seek water for them. 'Tis then he said, so that he might not have to go forth to seek the water:

Cold till Doom!
The storm is greater than ever;
Each shining furrow is a river,
And a full lake each ford.

Big as a great sea is each angry lake,
Each keen thin company a host,
When big as the face of a shield each drop of rain,
Big as a white wether's skin each flake.

Big as a pit each . . . puddle,
A standing-stone each level, a wood each moor;
No shelter find the flocks of birds,
White snow reaches right up to the breech.

Swift frost has bound the roads
After a sharp struggle round Colt's standing-stone;
The storm has spread on all sides,
So that none say aught but "Cold!"

KUNO MEYER

The Song of the Sea

A great storm has arisen on the plain of Ler,
. . . bold across its high shores,
the wind has arisen, the cruel winter has wounded us,
coming over the great shaggy sea.

    •   •   •   •   •

When the wind is from the East—
the spirit of the wave is aroused,
so that it strives to pass us westward
to the land where sets the sun,
  to the rough, broad, green sea.

When the wind blows from the North—
the harsh dark waves strive
to reach the southern world
waging war with the pale sky,
  listening to the . . . song.

When the wind blows from the West
over the swift streams of the sea—
it strives to go past us east
into the arrows of the sun . . .
  into the wide and distant sea.

When the wind blows from the South
across the firm-shields of the Saxons—
its waves strike the isle of Scit,
travels to the head of Calathnit,
  beating against grey-green Limerick.

The ocean is full, the tide is high,
the wherry-mansion is beautiful;
the sandstorm whirls
around the Estuary of the Two Showers,
    swift is the rudder against the broad sea.

.   .   .   .   .

The wave has tumbled, great its strength,
over each broad estuary,
the wind has come, pale winter has wounded us,
around Cantyre, around Scotland,
    from Sliabh Dremon pours a full stream.

Son of God the Father, with vast hosts,
save me from the terror of rough weather,
just Lord of the Feast,
but save me from the storm,
    from the dread tempest of Hell.

KUNO MEYER

The Blackbird's Nest

Sad is yonder blackbird's song,
Well I know what wrought it wrong;
Whosoe'er the deed has done,
Now its nestlings are all gone.

Such a sorrow I, too, know
For such loss, not long ago;
Well, O bird! I read thy state
For a home laid desolate.

How thy heart has burned, nigh broke,
At the rude and reckless stroke!
To lay waste thy little nest
Seems to cowboys but a jest.

Thy clear note called together
Flutt'ring young in new feather;
From thy nest comes now not one—
O'er its mouth the nettle's gone.

Sudden came the callous boys,
Their deed all thy young destroys:
Thou and I one fate deplore—
For my children are no more.

By thy side there used to be
Thy sweet mate from o'er the sea;
The herd's net ensnared her head—
She is gone from thee and dead.

O Ruler of high heaven!
Thou'st laid our loads uneven:
For our friends on every side
'Mid their mates and children bide.

Hither come hosts of Faery
To waste our homes unwary;
Though they left no wound to tell
Brunt of battles were less fell.

Woe for wife; for children, woe!
I, in sorrow's shadow, go;
Not a trace of them I had
Hence my heavy heart is sad.

GEORGE SIGERSON

Wood to Burn and Not to Burn

The fire-servant, as in Iubhdan's presence he was kindling a fire, threw upon it a woodbine that twined around a branch and this led Iubhdan to say:

O man that for Fergus of the feasts dost kindle fire,
Whether afloat or ashore burn not the king of woods.

Monarch of Innisfail's forests the woodbine is, whom none
  may hold captive;
No feeble sovereign's effort is it to hug all tough trees in his
  embrace.

The pliant woodbine if thou burn, wailings for misfortune
  will abound,
Dire extremity at weapons' points or drowning in great
  waves will follow.

Burn not the precious apple tree of spreading and low-
  sweeping bough;
Tree ever decked in bloom of white, against whose fair
  head all men put forth the hand.

The surly blackthorn is a wanderer, a wood that the artificer
  burns not;
Throughout his body, though it be scanty, birds in their
  flocks warble.

The noble willow burn not, a tree sacred to poems;
Within his bloom bees are a-sucking, all love the little cage.

The graceful tree with the berries, the wizards' tree, the
    rowan burn;
But spare the limber tree; burn not the slender hazel.

Dark is the colour of the ash; timber that makes the wheels
    to go;
Rods he furnishes for horsemen's hands, his form turns
    battle into flight.

Tenterhook among woods the spiteful brier is, burn him
    that is so keen and green;
He cuts, he flays the foot, him that would advance he
    forcibly drags backward.

Fiercest heat-giver of all timber is green oak, from him
    none may escape unhurt;
By partiality for him the head is set on aching, and by his
    acrid embers the eye is made sore.

Alder, very battle-witch of all woods, tree that is hottest
    in the fight—
Undoubtedly burn at thy discretion both the alder and
    whitethorn.

Holly, burn it green; holly, burn it dry;
Of all trees whatsoever the critically best is holly.

Elder that hath tough bark, tree that in truth hurts sore;
Him that furnishes horses to the armies from the sidh burn
so that he be charred.

The birch as well, if he be laid low, promises abiding
fortune;
Burn up most sure and certainly the stalks that bear the
constant pods.

Put on the hearth if it so please thee, the russet aspen to
come headlong down;
Burn, be it late or early, the tree with the palsied branch.

Patriarch of long-lasting woods is the yew, sacred to feasts
as is well known;
Of him now build ye dark-red vats of goodly size.

Ferdedh, thou faithful one, wouldst thou but do my behest:
To thy soul as to thy body, O man, 'twould work advantage.

STANDISH O'GRADY

Sea Snatches

I

It has broken us,
crushed us,
drowned us,
O King of the star-bright Kingdom of Heaven,
the wind has consumed us,
even as the blood-red lightning devours timber.

II

The harsh winter is here.
The water covers the flat land;
frosts have untied the leaves,
and the waves, until now merry,
begin to growl.

III

North East
behold ye,
far and wide,
the Irish Sea.

Monsters sport in it,
seals look over it.
Look, ye too!
It is full tide!

IV

What if the clouds are from the left!
Let us have courage; up from your knees;
twist the prow for Damietta,
the tiller to the bones of Greece.

[64]

What if the clouds are from the left!
Black wind howling out of Acras vile!
Come, O Magdalene! Lift
these clouds. Waft us to the Nile.

V

The white hair of the sea is shaken . . .
that wild wind means sleep for me;
tonight I fear no Viking raiders—
they will not brave the Irish Sea.

VI

It is Cascorach the Bloody, who killed
the woman. He let her lie—
her head upon the sand,
the foam about her thigh.

S. O'F.

The Drowning of Conaing

The shining waters rise and swell
And break across the shining strand,
And Conaing gazes at the land,
Swung high in his frail coracle.

Then she with the white hair of foam,
The blinding hair that Conaing grips,
Rises, to turn triumphant lips,
On all the gods that guard his home.

FRANK O'CONNOR

PART III

The Heroic Tradition

The Three Most Famous Tales

Three sorrows of story-telling fill me with pity,
the telling of them grates on the ear;
the woe of the Children of Tuireann—
sorrowful to hear.

And the Children of Lir, bird-shaped;
a curse on the mouth that told their doom:
Conn, Fiacra, Fionnuala, and Aodh—
the second gloom.

And the Children of Usna, shield of men,
who fell by force and cunning craft—
Naoisi, and Ainnle, and Ardan . . .
There cracks the heart.

S. O'F.

The Icebound Swans

Pitiful these crying swans tonight,
caught by the ebb, or is it drought?
Without water coldly flowing at their breasts,
they, three, must die of thirst.

Without water, the firm, thin, and strong,
beating on their breasts in waves;
the great, bubbling sea all gone—
they are held on the smooth, hard plain.

O King, who brought the tribes to liberty,
who formed heaven, who formed earth,
release, tonight, this little flock, these swans,
chastise the strong until they grow pitiful.

S. O'F.

Deirdre Looks Back at Scotland

Beloved to me is that land to the East,
Alba with its marvels,
I would not have come hither from it
if I were not come with Naoisi.

Beloved to me Dun Fidga and Dun Finn,
beloved the dun above them,
beloved Inis Draigen
and beloved Dun Sweeney.

Caill Cuan!
whither Ainnle would go, alas!
I thought the time passed swiftly there,
I and Naoisi in Scotland.

Glen Laid!
I used to sleep there under the white rocks,
fish and flesh and rich badger,
was my share in Glen Laid.

Glen Masain!
tall its wild garlic, white its stalks,
we slept uneasily
over the rough estuary of Masain.

Glen Eitchi!
There I raised my first house,
delightful its wood, after rising,
a pen for the sun was Glen Eitchi.

[71]

Glen Urchan!
That was the straight, fair-ridged hill,
no man of his age was prouder
than Naoisi in Glen Urchan.

Glen Da Ruadh!
Welcome every man who has a right to it,
sweet is the cuckoo on the bending branch,
on the peak above Glen Da Ruadh.

Beloved is Draigen and its firm strand,
beloved its water in pure sand:
I would not have come from the East
if I were not to come with my lover.

S. O'F.

Deirdre's Lament over Naoisi

Long is the day without Usnech's children:
It was not mournful to be in their company,
Sons of a king, by whom pilgrims were rewarded,
Three lions from the Hill of the Cave!

Three dragons of Dun Monaid,
The three champions from the Red Branch:
After them I am not alive:
Three that used to break every onrush.

Three darlings of the women of Britain,
Three hawks of Slieve Gullion,
Sons of a king whom valour served,
To whom soldiers used to give homage.

Three heroes who were not good at homage,
Their fall is cause of sorrow—
Three sons of Cathbad's daughter,
Three props of the battalion of Cuilgne.

Three vigorous bears,
Three lions out of Lis Una,
Three heroes who loved their praise,
The three sons of the breast of the Ulstermen.

Three who were fostered by Aoife,
To whom a district was under tribute:
Three columns of breach of battle,
Three fosterlings whom Scathach had.

Three who were reared by Boghmhain.
At learning every feat;
Three renowned sons of Usnech:
It is mournful to be absent from them.

That I should remain after Naoisi
Let no one in the world suppose:
After Ardan and Ainnle
My time would not be long.

Ulster's overking, my first husband,
I forsook for Naoisi's love:
Short my life after them:
I will perform their funeral game.

After them I will not be alive—
Three that would go into every conflict,
Three who liked to endure hardships,
Three heroes who refused not combats.

A curse on thee. O wizard Cathbad,
Thou slewest Naoisi through a woman!
Sad that there was none to help him,
The one king that satisfies the world!

O man that diggest the tomb,
And that puttest my darling from me,
Make not the grave too narrow:
I shall be beside the noble ones.

WHITLEY STOKES

Deirdre and Conchobar

Though you think beautiful the valiant champions
who come into Emain after a march,
more beautiful was the march from their house
of the three heroic sons of Usnech:

Naoisi making mead of delicious hazelnuts,
bathing with me beside the fire,
Ardan with an ox or a fat hog,
Ainnle's shoulder-bundle of faggots over the high-river.

Though you think sweet the rich mead
that Mac Nessa of the great battles drinks,
I have known ere now a chase upon a doe
the food of which was many times more sweet.

When Naoisi the noble would set
a mess on the faggots of the wild-plain,
sweeter was all food than honey;
the son of Usnech had chosen it.

Though you think sweet in every month
pipers and trumpeters,
I pledge my conscience this day
that I have heard music more sweet.

The heavy wave-voice of Naoisi,
was music always sweet to hear:
Ardan's string-music was good,
Ainnle humming toward his wild hut.

[75]

Do not break this day my heart—
soon shall I reach my early grave.
Sorrow is more powerful than the sea,
if you but knew it, O Conchobar.

Eugene O'Curry

The Sleep-Song for Diarmuid

Sleep a little, a little little,
thou needst not feel or fear or dread,
lad to whom I give my love,
Son of O'Duibhne—Diarmuid.

Sleep here soundly, sweetly sleep,
noble Diarmuid O'Duibhne,
I shall be thy watchman, here,
dear, gracious Diarmuid.

Sleep, little lamb, a little
above this well of Trengort;
blessings on you, lakeside lamb,
wombed in a great river-land.

Sleep the southern sleep
of the high-poet Dedach
when he fled with the daughter of Morann
in spite of Conall of the Red Branch.

Or sleep the sleep of Assaroe
the northern sleep of fair and comely Finncha,
when he fled with Slaine of the heavy lids,
in spite of Falvey Hardhead.

Sleep the little western sleep
that slept Gailian's daughter, Aine,
after her flight by torch-light
with Duvach from Derinish.

[77]

Or let it be like Degha's sleep
when, bold, and proud, he lay in sleep
with Coicheann, child of Binn,
in spite of Dechill of Dhurinn.

O fold of all the valour west of Greece,
for whom I wake, thy watchman,
my heart will come near breaking
if there come a time when I see thee not.

It would be the parting of the children of one home,
it would be the parting of body and soul—
my heir of the fair land of Loch Carman—
the parting of two lovers such as us.

The stag is not asleep in the east,
he never ceases belling,
although he is cosy in the blackbirds' wood,
he has no mind for sleep.

Why is not the hornless doe asleep,
calling for her speckled calf?
Running over the tops of the bushes;
she cannot sleep in her lair.

The linnet is awake and twittering
above the tips of the swaying trees:
they are all chattering in the woods—
and even the thrush is not asleep.

[78]

Why does not the wild duck sleep,
not sleep, nor drowse,
why does it not sleep in its nest,
swimming steadily with all its strength?

Tonight the grouse does not sleep
above the high, stormy, heathery hill;
sweet the cry of her clear throat,
sleepless among the streams.

Caoilte, O Diarmuid, is loosed on thy track.
Caoilte's running will not take him astray.
May nor death nor dishonour touch thee—
but leave thee in an everlasting sleep. . . .

S. O'F.

Lament for Cael

The haven roars, and O, the haven roars,
over the rushing race of Rinn-da-bharc:
the drowning of the warrior of Lach-da-conn,
that is what the wave beating on the strand laments.

Sweet the calling crane, and O, sweet the calling crane,
in the marshlands of Druim-da-thren:
'tis she that may not save her brood alive,
the wild dog of two colours is intent on her nestlings.

A woeful note, and O, a note of woe,
the thrush makes in Druim-cain,
and no cheerful note
the blackbird makes in Letterlee.

A woeful sound, and O, a woeful sound,
the deer makes in Druim-da-heish:
dead lies the doe of Druim Sileann,
the mighty stag bells after her.

Sore suffering to me
the death of the hero who used to lie with me,
that the son of the woman out of Doire-da-dos
should be with a trestle under his head.

Sore suffering to me is Cael,
that he should be in the shape of Death by my side:
that a wave should have swept over his white side,
that is what has distracted me, remembering the joy of him.

A dismal roar, and O, a dismal roar,
the shore surf makes against the strand,
for that it has engulfed the comely, noble man—
sorrow that Cael ever encountered it.

A woeful booming, and O, a woeful booming,
the wave makes upon the Northward beach
butting against the polished rock
wailing for Cael who has gone from me.

A woeful fight, and O, a fight of woe,
the wave makes with the Southward beach:
as for me—my span is declared,
the passing of my beauty is known to all men.

A woeful melody
the heavy surge of Tulach-leis does make:
as for me—I have nothing,
the story that has wounded me has crushed me.

Now that Crimhthann's son is drowned
none that I might love lives after:
many a chief fell by his hand
and in battle his shield never cried for being struck.

S. O'F.

Conall's Head

Ochagon!—here is the head
Of Conall of the keen blue blade:
The head of understanding clear,
The noble, dear, devoted head.

Ochagon! here are the eyes
Of Conall's wise and generous head;
From these the lashes used to rise
And flashes mild and manly sped.

Ochagon! here is the mouth
That north and south the poets praise,
Of slender grace and apple-red,
Like honey shed was Conall's mouth.

Ochagon! here is the hand
Bore Conall son of Scanlan's brand,
The hand that strong in conflict strove,
The hand of Conall—my first love!

Ochagon! here is the side
Where oftentimes ours nobly lay;
From Moyle's grey tide there came a hound
With wile to wound that stainless side.

Ochagon! here are the feet
That ne'er gave way where warriors meet:
Feet still first in fiery fray,
The battle bravest Conall's feet!

Och! and here his Fort for aye,
The strong cold Clay for all the years,
Conall's fort—where I deplore
Whose tale is o'er—the House of Tears!

George Sigerson

Cuchulainn's Lament for Ferdiad

Play was each, pleasure each,
Till Ferdiad faced the beach;
One had been our student life,
One in strife of school our place,
One our gentle teacher's grace
   Loved o'er all and each.

Play was each, pleasure each,
Till Ferdiad faced the beach;
One had been our wonted ways,
One the praise for feat of fields,
Scathach gave two victor shields
   Equal prize to each.

Play was each, pleasure each,
Till Ferdiad faced the beach;
Dear that pillar of pure gold
Who fell cold beside the ford.
Hosts of heroes felt his sword
   First in battle's breach.

Play was each, pleasure each,
Till Ferdiad faced the beach;
Lion fiery, fierce and bright,
Wave whose might no thing withstands,
Sweeping, with the shrinking sands,
   Horror o'er the beach.

Play was each, pleasure each,
Till Ferdiad faced the beach;
Loved Ferdiad, dear to me:
I shall dree his death for aye—
Yesterday a Mountain he,
    A Shade today.

GEORGE SIGERSON

Fand Yields Cuchulainn to Emer

Emer, he is your man, now,
and well may you wear him,
when I can no longer hold him,
I must yield him.

Many a man has wanted me,
but I have kept my vows.
I have been an honest woman,
under the roofs and boughs.

Pity the woman loves a man,
when no love invites her.
Better for her to fly from love
if unloved, love bites her.

S. O'F.

The Fairy Midir's Invitation to Etain

Befind, wilt thou not come with me,
into my sweet land, to all its wonders,
where every poll is like a primrose,
every body the whiteness of snow?

There is no thine, or mine, in that land,
where teeth are white, eyebrows jet,
eyes shining—great their host—
and each cheek bright as the foxglove.

However heady the ale of Inish Fail,
the ale of that Great Land is more heady still;
it is a marvel of lands, that land of which I speak,
and there young men never grow old.

On every side we see everyone.
No one sees us.
We are hidden from their spying
by the gloom of (their) Adam's sin.

Woman, if you join my strong people,
there will be gold on your head,
O lovely one, you will have with me
fresh swine-flesh, new milk, ales to drink,

warm, sweet streams across the land,
choice of mead and wine,
perfect comrades without a stain.
And without sin we shall conceive, nor lust.

S. O'F.

[87]

Recollections of Oisin

I remember a day, and if it were then,
you would come to me before any other man,
and you would wash my two hands,
O woman. You would not avoid me, then.

My quiet, fair-haired girl,
it is a pity you did not
wash my poor bald pate for burial
and lay me under the cold cairn.

Fine was the beauty of the fair hair
that all men saw on my head, then,
but it has left me for good and all,
and I am a sick-faced grey-pate.

Fine and lustrous was my hair,
a fine crown for a body;
no better hair, but Fionn's alone,
ever grew through the skull of a man.

Aye, and these teeth up here,
away up in my old head, now,
they were another wonder—
they would crunch the yellow-topped nuts.

They would gnaw the haunch of a stag,
hard, and hungry, and hound-like;
they would not leave a jot or joint
that they would not make mince-meat of it.

And these eyes up here,
deep now in my old skull,
tonight mere roots of blood,
they were, once, clean, pearly gems.

Tonight, if I looked out the window,
I would not see the crowded fair.
Once, on a night of black, blind weather,
they would not lead me a step astray.

And these legs under me,
nothing could tire them—once.
Tonight, look at them, bandy and bent,
miserable, skinny.

They have neither power nor vigour,
I can barely stir them.
They were swift, at one time,
following the shade of yellow Fionn.

S. O'F.

Recollections of Caoilte

*Upon the whole province, now, distress of cold settled
and heavy snow came down so that it reached men's shoulders and chariots' axle-trees, and of the forest's russet
branches made a twisting together as if it had been of
withes, so that men might not travel there. Caoilte then said,
a fitting time it is now for wild stags and does to seek the
topmost points of hills and rocks, a timely season for salmon
to betake themselves into the cavities of the banks. And then
he uttered a lay:*

Cold is the winter, the wind has arisen,
the courageous, unquelled stag is up:
not tonight is the whole hill warm,
yet for all that the wild stag bells.

He does not lie upon his side,
the deer of the hill of Carn na Comhdál:
no less than he does the stag of the tip of icy Echtge
hear the bellow of the wolf-pack.

I, Caoilte, and brown Diarmuid,
and keen, light Oscar
would listen to the music of the pack
in the waning end of the cold night.

Well sleeps the brown stag,
his fur pressed to a rock—
he might be under the surface of the earth
this waning end of the cold night.

Today I am an old man
knowing but a few living men:
yet I used of a time shake a sharp spear,
in the cold ice-bound mornings.

To Heaven's King I offer thanks,
to Mary the Virgin's son:
time was I used quieten a whole host—
they, at least, are colder than I am tonight.

S. O'F.

The Blackbird of Derrycairn

Oisin to Saint Patrick:

Sweetly sung, O blackbird of Derrycairn,
I have heard in no quarter of the world
music sweeter than your call
as you nestle in the depths of the tree.

Foolish who does not listen for a while
to the sweetest music on earth:
Mac Calpurn of the sweet bells,
you can return after a while to your prayers.

If you knew the bird's tale,
then you even as I,
would weep bitterly
and forget your God for a while.

In Norway of the blue waters
Mac Cumhall of the golden horns found
this bird you are watching now—
that truly is its history.

Derrycairn, the western wood
where the Fian used to rest—
there, for the beauty and the grace of its trees
the blackbird was nested.

[92]

The call of the blackbird of Derrycairn,
the belling of the stag from Caill-na-gCaor,
that is the music to which Finn found early sleep,
and the wild duck of Loch-na-dTri-Caol.

The grouse in Cruachan Cuinn,
the otter whistling in Druim da Loch,
the eagle crying in Gleann-na-bFuath,
the laughter of the cuckoo in Cnoc-na-Scoth,

The dogs barking from Gleann Caoin,
the scream of the eagle from Cnoc-na-Sealg,
the pattering of the dogs returning early
home from the Strand of the Red Stones . . .

Ah, when Finn and the Fian lived,
they loved better the mountain than the monastery:
sweet to them was the blackbird's speech.
As for your bells' tongues—they despised them!

S. O'F.

Eve's Lament

I am Eve—great Adam's wife,
it was I who cheated Jesus of old,
it was I who robbed my children of heaven,
I by right should have been stretched on the cross.

I had a kingly house at my pleasure,
evil the choice that disgraced me,
evil the crooked word that withered me,
alas! my hand is unclean.

It was I who took down the apple
that went beyond the narrows of my gullet;
as long as they live in this life,
not a breath will women change from folly.

There would have been ice in no place,
there would be no windy, glistering winter,
there would be no hell, no sorrow,
no terror—were it not for me!

S. O'F.

Love Epigram

The son of the King of the River Muad,
in midsummer,
found a maiden in a greenwood:
she gave him blackberries
from the bushes,
and as love-token,
strawberries on a rush-tip.

S. O'F.

Liadain and Cuirithir

Liadain had loved Cuirithir, and then taken the veil.
Afterwards she felt the agony of love and went seeking him.
When he heard she was coming from the West he went in
a coracle on the sea and took to strange lands and pilgrimage
so that they never met again. Then it may be that she said
this poem. They say that she was on the flagstone where he
used to pray until she died, and that stone was placed on her
grave:

A vain thing
is the thing that I have done
so a lover's heart to wring.

Mad beyond measure
(but for the wrath of God between)
she who would have done his pleasure.

I am she,
Liadain that loved Cuirithir,
as you murmur, watching me.

It was I,
that in company with him
saw so good a time go by.

Woods woke
to music when he walked with me,
and for me the blue sea spoke.

Would to God
naught had made him wrath with me
of all things I ever did.

Do not hide
the great love I had for him,
more than all things else beside.

Flames shake
so my sorry heart for him
that without him it must break. . . .

FRANK O'CONNOR

The Tryst with Death

The lover, having been intercepted by his enemies, keeps his promise to his mistress, saying:

Woman, speak not with me!
my thoughts are not on thee,
my thoughts are still entangled
in the fight at Féic.

My bloodstained corpse lies
by the side of the Slope of two Banks,
and my unwashed head
sleeps among soldiers in the trampled field.

Foolish restraint for anyone given to trysting
to postpone the tryst with death;
the tryst I made at Clarach,
I keep, in pallor.

It was fated for me, unhappy my fight;
at Féic my grave has been marked out;
my lot has been marked out, wretched fight,
to die by the youths of another land.

I am not the only man in the heat of desire
to go trysting with a woman;
it is not to reproach thee, though it was for thee I came.
Pitiful is our final trysting, here.

I came from afar to our trysting,
which was so hateful to our noble friend;
had we known it would end thus
it would have been easy not to persist.

It was a merry graceful company
up to the hour of their death:
the green-leaved wood has gathered them in—
it was a wholly terrifying slaughter.

Great my agony of thirst—
farewell for ever to flowing plenty—
I thought indeed that thou wouldst come to me
though thou didst not promise it.

Do not stay this dread night,
on the plain among the graves of the dead pack;
it is not worth a woman's while to sleep with a corpse.
. . . take my spoils.

It will shine before you, a coloured gem,
the white cup of my cupbearer,
my golden ring, my bracelets, treasures without a blemish,
brought me by Nia Nar from over the sea.

And Caoilte's brooch—a lucky pin—
one of his famous treasures—
two silver hounds after a golden hound,
it is a good piece though small.

Quickly unclasp, it was the end of the bloodletting,
the bronze collar about my neck;
all of them—noble spoils—
lie where my body fell.

There are about us
many spoils famous for their luck;
fearsome the monstrous entrails
the Morrigan washes.

She has come from the mouth of the grave,
it is she who incited us,
many a spoil she washes,
evil the twisted laugh she laughs.

My riddled body must part with thee for a while,
my soul to be tortured by the demon.
Love of this life is folly,
but for the adoring of the King of Heaven.

It is the dusky raven that laughs
his greeting to all the faithful—
a ghost is my speech and my face . . .
O woman! Do not speak to me!

S. O'F.

The Hag of Beare

In a nunnery she weeps and says:

Ebbtide with me, as with the sea;
old-age has made me yellow:
though I do penance for it,
it is well my doom has come.

I am the old Hag of Beare,
I used to wear the freshest linen,
today, old and worn,
I have not even a second shift.

It is money
ye love, not men:
the days when I lived
it was men we loved.

They were loved men
of whose lands we had the run:
well we lived with them
and little did they boast of it after.

But today they ask with fair words
and little the bounty given:
and though it is little that is given
greatly they boast of it after.

O the swift chariots,
and the horses bearing off the victory!
They had their floodtide—
a blessing on the noble who gave them to me.

My wretched body has come
to its proper refuge now:
when the Son of God deems it time
let him come to deliver his command.

When my arms are seen
they are bony and thin:
time was when they made love for me
around glorious kings.

When my arms are seen
they are bony and thin,
they are not fit, I declare,
to lift above fair youths.

The girls are all happy
when May day comes to them:
fitter for me to weep
for I am a pitiful old woman.

No more the sweet gossip,
the wethers are no longer killed for my wedding,
scant and grey my hair,
the miserable veil over it is no shame.

I care nothing
that a white veil should be on my head—
many a coloured mether-cup
I raised above my head as I drank the good ale.

I envy no old thing
save only the plain of Femon:
here am I spent by the storms
and the yellow crops still blow on Femon.

But the stones of the kings on Femon,
and the chair of Ronan on Bregon—
it is long since the storms reached them
and made old, withered cheeks of them.

The wave of the great sea talks loudly,
the winter has come:
Fermuid the son of Mugh—
I do not expect him on a visit today.

I know what they are doing,
they row and row
through the reeds of the Ford of Allen—
cold the dwelling where they sleep.

It's "O my day,"
that not a child of them lives rowing about,
and my shape changed this many a year
and my youthful energy all gone.

Today it's "O my God"
with me—whatever will come of it;
even in the hot sun I must wear my shift.
The time is coming that will reshape me.

Youth's Summer that we once had
I have spent and its Autumn:
Winter-age that spends all men
has come to me.

First I spent my youth,
I am glad to have done with it;
and if my leap be small now, by Dua!
I have worn my cloak well.

Beautiful the green cloak
that my lord loved across my shoulders:
it was a noble man who loved it
and put new fur on it when it was bare.

Amen! Woe is me!
Every acorn has to drop.
After feasting by shining candles,
to be in the gloom of a nunnery!

I had my day with kings,
drinking mead and wine,
today I drink whey-water
among withered old women.

Let my wine-goblets be cups of whey,
at the will of God every hour;
I pray thee, O living God,
who wast slain in anger.

On my cloak I see the hair of age—
my reason deceives me—
it is the grey hair growing through my skin,
the truth is, I am an old woman.

My right eye has been taken from me,
sold in fee-simple,
and the left has been taken from me
to increase the already too-great forfeiture.

The floodtide
and the two great ebbtides!
What the wave gives in flood,
the backwash snatches from your hand.

The floodtide
and the second ebbtide!
They have all reached me,
I know them well.

The floodtide
will not reach the silence of my cell:
though many my company in the dark
—the hand of death has touched them all.

If the Son of Mary knew
that I am under the rooftree of my cell—
though I have not shown Him hospitality before
He has never refused anyone.

Sad all creatures,
and beyond all one creature,
that I saw not this ebb
when I saw the flood.

My floodtide!
how well I remember it!
Jesus the Son of Mary has saved me
so that I weary for the ebb.

Happy the island of the great sea,
which the flood reaches after the ebb,
whereas I cannot expect
the flood to reach me after the ebb.

There is scarcely a little spot today
That I can recall to memory:
what was on flood
is all gone. . . .   S. O'F.

Sweeney the Mad

Sweeney was a king in Northern Ireland who fled in madness from battle hiding with the wild birds in the trees of Ireland. The medieval romance of Sweeney the Mad tells that:

. . . when he arrived out of the battle, it was seldom that his feet would touch the ground because of the swiftness of his course, and when he did touch it, he would not shake the dew from the top of the grass for the lightness and nimbleness of his step. He halted not from that headlong course until he left neither plain, nor field, nor bare mountain, nor bog, nor thicket, nor marsh, nor hill, nor hollow, nor dense-sheltering wood in Ireland that he did not travel that day, until he reached Ros Bearaigh, in Glenn Earcain, where he went into the yew tree that was in the glen.

Suibhne had a kinsman in the battle, to wit Aongus the Stout, who came in flight with a number of his people out of the battle, and the route he took was through Glenn Earcain.

Now when Sweeney heard the shout of the multitude and the tumult of the great army, he ascended from the tree towards the rainclouds of the firmament, over the summits of every place and over the ridgepole of every land. For a long time thereafter he was (faring) throughout Ireland, visiting and searching in hard, rocky clefts and in bushy branches of tall ivy-trees, in narrow cavities of stones, from estuary to estuary, from peak to peak, and from glen to glen, till he reached ever-delightful Glen Bolcain. It is there the madmen of Ireland used to go when their year in madness was complete, that glen being ever a place of great delight for the crazy. Sweeney also remained for a long time in the glen until he happened one night to be on the top of

*a tall ivyclad hawthorn tree which was in the glen. It was
hard for him to endure that bed, for at every twist and turn
he would give, a shower of thorns off the hawthorn would
stick to him, so that they were piercing and rending his
side and wounding his skin. Sweeney thereupon changed
from that bed to another place, where there was a dense
thicket of great briers with fine thorns, and a single protrud-
ing branch of blackthorn growing alone up through the
thicket. Sweeney settled on the top of that tree, but so slender was it that it bowed and bent under him, so that he
fell heavily through the thicket to the ground, and there
was not as much as an inch from his sole to the crown of
his head that was not wounded and reddened.*

*In that wise he remained in Glen Bolcain until at a cer-
tain time he raised himself (into the air) and went to Cluain
Cille in the border of Tir Conaill and Tir Boghaine. He
went then to the brink of the well where he had for food
that night watercress and water. Thereafter he went into
the old tree of the church. That night there came an exceed-
ing great storm so that the extent of the night's misery affected Suibhne greatly, and he said:*

I

Cold is the snow tonight,
lasting now is my poverty,
there is no strength in me for fight,
famine has wounded me, madman as I am.

All men see that I am not shapely,
bare of thread is my tattered garment,

Suibhne of Ros Earcain is my name,
the crazy madman am I.

I rest not when night comes,
my foot frequents no trodden way,
I bide not here for long,
the bonds of terror come upon me.

My goal lies beyond the teeming main,
voyaging the prow-abounding sea;
fear has laid hold of my poor strength
I am the crazy one of Glen Bolcain.

Frosty wind tearing me,
already snow has wounded me,
the storm bearing me to death
from the branches of each tree.

Grey branches have wounded me,
they have torn my hands;
the briers have not left
the making of a girdle for my feet.

There is a palsy on my hands,
everywhere there is cause of confusion
From Sliabh Mis to Sliabh Cuillenn,
from Sliabh Cuillenn to Cuialgne.

Sad for ever is my cry
on the summit of Cruachan Aighle,
from Glen Bolcain to Islay,
from Cenn Tire to Boirche.

Small is my portion when day comes,
it comes not as a new day's right (?)
a tuft of watercress of Cluain Cille
with Cell Cua's cuckoo flower.

He who is at Ros Earcach,
neither trouble nor evil shall come to him;
that which makes me strengthless
is being in snow in nakedness.

II

But when Sweeney had been hiding for a fortnight in the old yew tree of Ros Earcain, his people took counsel of one another and everyone said that Loingseachan (Lynchehaun) should be sent to lure him home; so that Loingseachan went and said to him:

Loingseachan:
O Suibhne from lofty Sliabh na nEach,
thou of the rough blade wert given to wounding;
for Christ's sake, who hath put thee in bondage,
grant converse with thy foster-brother.

Hearken to me if thou hearest me,
O splendid king, O great prince,
so that I may relate gently
to thee tidings of thy good land.

There is life for none in thy land after thee;
it is to tell of it that I have come;
dead is thy renowned brother there,
dead is thy father and thy mother.

Suibhne:

If my gentle mother be dead,
harder is it for me to go to my land;
'tis long since she has loved my body;
she has ceased to pity me.

Foolish the counsel for each wild youth
whose elders live not;
like unto a branch bowed under nuts;
whoso is brotherless has a gaping side.

Loingseachan:

There is another calamity there
which is bewailed by the men of Erin,
though uncouth be thy side and thy foot,
dead is thy fair wife of grief for thee.

Suibhne:

For a household to be without a wife
is rowing a rudderless boat,
'tis a garb of feathers to the skin,
'tis kindling a single fire.

Loingseachan:

I have heard a fearful and loud tale
around which was a clear, fierce wail,
'tis a fist round smoke, however,
thou art without sister, O Suibhne.

Suibhne:

A proverb this, bitter the . . .
it has no delight for me—
the mild sun rests on every ditch,
a sister loves though she be not loved.

Loingseachan:
Calves are not let to cows
amongst us in cold Araidhe
since thy gentle daughter who has loved thee died,
likewise thy sister's son.

Suibhne:
My sister's son and my hound,
they would not forsake me for wealth;
'tis adding loss to sorrow;
the heart's needle is an only daughter.

Loingseachan:
There is another famous story—
loath am I to tell it—
meetly are the men of the Arada
bewailing thy only son.

Suibhne:
That is the renowned drop (?)
which brings a man to the ground,
that his little son who used to say "daddy"
should be without life.

It has called me to thee from the tree,
scarce have I caused enmity,
I cannot bear up against the blow
since I heard the tidings of my only son.

When Sweeney was tempted from the trees by Lynchehaun's lies about his little son the madman became sane again. But one day they left him alone in Lynchehaun's bedroom with an old mill-hag who asked him to tell her some of the adventures of his years of madness. Fearing that madness might come on him again he raged at her:

"O hag," said he, "great are the hardships I have encountered if you but knew; many a dreadful leap have I leaped from hill to hill, from fortress to fortress, from land to land, from valley to valley." "For God's sake," said the hag, "leap for us now one of the leaps you used to leap when you were mad." Thereupon he bounded over the bedrail so that he reached the end of the bench. "My conscience!" said the hag, "I could leap that myself," and in the same manner she did so. He took another leap out through the skylight of the hostel. "I could leap that too," said the hag, and straightway she leaped. This, however, is a summary of it: Suibhne travelled through five cantreds of Dal Araidhe that day until he arrived at Glenn na nEachtach in Fiodh Gaibhle, and she followed him all that time. When Suibhne rested there on the summit of a tall ivy-branch, the hag rested on another tree beside him. It was then the end of harvest-time precisely. Thereupon Suibhne heard a hunting-call of a multitude in the verge of the wood. "This," said he, "is the cry of a great host, and they are the Ui Faelain, whom I slew in the battle of Magh Rath." He heard the bellowing of the stag, and he made a lay wherein he eulogized aloud the trees of Ireland, and recalling some of his own hardships and sorrows, he said:

O little stag, thou little bleating one,
O melodious little clamourer,
sweet to us is the music
thou makest in the glen.

Longing for my little home
has come on my senses—
the flocks in the plain,
the deer on the mountain.

Thou oak, bushy, leafy,
thou art high beyond trees;
O hazlet, little branching one,
O fragrance of hazelnuts.

O alder, thou art not hostile,
delightful is thy hue,
thou art not rending and prickling
in the gap wherein thou art.

O little blackthorn, little thorny one;
O little black sloe-tree;
O watercress, little green-topped one,
from the brink of the ousel(?) spring.

O minen of the pathway,
thou art sweet beyond herbs,
O little green one, very green one,
O herb on which grows the strawberry.

O apple tree, little apple tree,
much art thou shaken;
O quicken, little berried one,
delightful is thy bosom.

O brier, little arched one,
thou grantest no fair terms,
thou ceasest not to tear me
till thou hast thy fill of blood.

O yew tree, little yew tree,
in churchyards thou art conspicuous;
O ivy, little ivy,
thou art familiar in the dusky wood.

O holly, little sheltering one,
thou door against the wind;
O ash tree, thou baleful one,
hand-weapon of a warrior.

O birch, smooth and blessed,
thou melodious, proud one,
delightful each entwining branch
in the top of thy crown.

The aspen a-trembling;
by turns I hear
its leaves a-racing
meseems 'tis the foray!

My aversion in woods—
I conceal it not from anyone—
is the leafy stirk of an oak
swaying evermore.(?)

A proud ivy-bush
which grows through a twisted tree
if I were right on its summit,
I would fear to come out.

I flee before the skylarks,
'tis a stern, great race;
I leap over the stumps
on the tops of the mountains.

When the proud turtle-dove
rises for us,
quickly do I overtake it
since my feathers have grown.

The silly, foolish woodcock,
when it rises for me,
methinks 'tis a bitter foe;
the blackbird, too, that gives the cry of alarm.

Every time I would bound
till I was on the ground
so that I might see the little fox
below a-gnawing the bones.

Beyond every wolf(?) among the ivy-trees
swiftly would he get the advantage of me,
so nimbly would I leap
till I was on the mountain-peak.

Little foxes yelping
to me and from me,
wolves at their rending,
I flee at their sound.

They have striven to reach me,
coming in their swift course,
so that I fled before them
to the tops of the mountains.

There will come the starry frost
which will fall on every pool;
I am wretched, straying,
exposed to it on the mountain-peak.

The herons a-calling
in chilly Glenn Aighle,
swift flocks of birds
coming and going.

I love not the merry prattle
that men and women make:
sweeter to me is the warbling
of the blackbirds in the quarter in which it is.

I love not the trumpeting
I hear at early morn:
sweeter to me the squeal
of the badgers in Benna Broc.

I love not the horn-blowing
so boldly I hear:
sweeter to me the belling of a stag
of twice twenty peaks.

There is the material of a plough-team
from glen to glen:
each stag at rest
on the summit of the peaks.

Though many are my stags
from glen to glen,
not often is a ploughman's hand
closing round their horns.(?)

The stag of lofty Sliabh Eibhlinne,
the stag of sharp Sliabh Fuaid,
the stag of Ealla, the stag of Orrery,
the fierce stag of Loch Lein.

The stag of Seimhne, Larne's stag,
the stag of Line of the mantles,
the stag of Cuialgne, the stag of Conachail,
the stag of Bairenn of the two peaks.

O mother of this herd,
thy coat has become grey,
there is no stag after thee
without twoscore antler-points.

Greater than the material for a little cloak
thy head has turned grey;
if I were on each little point,
there would be a pointlet on every point.

Thou stag that comest lowing
to me across the glen,
pleasant is the place for seats
on the top of thy antler-points.

I am Suibhne, a poor suppliant,
swiftly do I race across the glen;
that is not my lawful name,
rather is it Fer Benn.

The springs I found best:
the well of Leithead Lan,
the well most beautiful and cool
the fountain of Dun Mail.

Though many are my wanderings,
my raiment today is scanty;
I myself keep my watch
on the top of the mountains.

O tall, russet fern,
thy mantle has been made red;
there is no bed for an outlaw
in the branches of thy crests.

The curse of Ronan Finn
has thrown me in thy company,
O little stag, little bleating one,
O melodious little clamourer.

*After that lay, Suibhne came from Fiodh Gaibhle to Benn
Boghaine, thence to Benn Faibhne, thence to Rath Mur-
builg, but he found no refuge from the hag until he reached
Dun Sobairce in Ulster. Suibhne leaped from the summit
of the fort sheer down in front of the hag. She leaped
quickly after him, but dropped on the cliff of Dun Sobairce,
where she was broken to pieces, and fell into the sea. In
that manner she found death in the wake of Suibhne.*

J. G. O'KEEFFE

Aran

Aran of the many stags;
the washing of the sea against her side;
island where companies are fed,
ridge where blue spears are blooded.

Shy deer on her peaks,
soft berries in her heather,
icy water in her rivers,
mast on her brown oaks.

There are greyhounds and beagles,
blackberries and blackthorn sloes,
her homes are close under her woods,
deer wander through her oak-forests.

Scarlet gatherings on her rocks,
faultless grass on her slopes,
among her fair shapely herds
the lowing of the speckled leaping calves.

Smooth her plain, fat her swine,
pleasant are her fields—who doubts it?—
her nuts on the tops of her hazelwood,
the firm ships sailing by her.

It is delightful for them when the fine weather comes,
trout under the banks of her rivers,
seagulls answer around her bright cliff—
delightful at all times is Aran!

S. O'F.

Mananaan to Bran

A wondrous beauty, thinks Bran,
as he sails in his coracle over the shining sea!
To me, afar in my chariot
it is a flowering plain he rides upon.

What is a shining sea
for Bran's beaked coracle
is a fair plain of many blossoms
for my two-wheeled chariot.

Bran sees a host of breaking waves
over the bright sea;
but I see on this Plain of Sports
flawless, scarlet-headed blossoms.

There where Bran directs his glances
sea-horses glisten in summertime.
In the kingdom of Mananaan mac Lir
rivers gush forth their honeyed streams.

The colour of the sea where thou art,
the brightness of the ocean whereon thou rowest,
is earth, smooth land,
spread all about in yellow and blue.

Speckled salmon leap from the womb
of the fair waters *thou* seest;
they are calves, they are glittering lambs,
playing in friendly frolic.

Though thou seest but one charioteer
in the Fair Plain, with all its blossoms,
there are many horses on its surface,
unseen by thee.

The length of the plain, the extent of the host,
shines in colours of pure glory;
a fair stream of silver, steps of gold,
welcome every wanderer.

They play over the heady wine,
a pleasant game,
men and gentle women under the trees,
without evil or sin.

It has floated along the top of a wood,
thy coracle, and over hill-tops;
this beneath the prow of thy little boat
is a wood in fair fruit,

a wood, in blossom and in fruit,
overhung by the veritable vapour of wine,
a wood without nor decay, nor lack,
in leaf of coloured gold.

Here we are from the beginning of the creation
free of age, free of the declension of youth;
distress we expect not of it,
sin has not visited us.

Therefore steadily let Bran row;
it is not far to Land of Women;
Evin of great hospitality
he will reach before sunset.

S. O'F.

PART IV

Early Court Verse

On the Breaking-Up of a School

Tonight the schools disperse,
thereby are beds left widowed,
the folk of each bed will shed tears
at parting.

Many lay down, how sad,
last night, in the home where I dwelt,
although this eve they are more likely
to watch than to lie down.

The glory of the home I dwelt in,
O God, I see naught
so inglorious today;
it is a sermon to one who could understand.

The men of art had ever
a tryst against All Hallowtide:
were but one man living
their departure would be no dispersal.

O ye who were in his dwelling
in quest of art and residence,
well might ye loathe to hear
the utterance of the cuckoos.

When the school dispersed
each man of art went to his own homeland:
none cometh since then from his father's house
in quest of art.

Long seemed to me until dispersal of the school
that I saw by Ferghal's side:
longer than the dispersal of the school
is it to have lost my teacher's kindness.

It were easier for them to separate
than to seek a teacher in his stead:
it is a doom of captivity, O God, to his pupil
if he be with a strange teacher.

For thirty years
or longer, I bear witness,
I was full of my breath from pride
until anguish came to cool me.

My prowess in his banqueting hall
has been punished by draughts of sorrow:
if I have lived riotously, O God,
the punishment is sorer.

For my training he would not have
me one night away from him,
till he loosed me against the birds
I was ever in one hut with O'Huiginn.

A reproach against me, to my hurt,
made in secret to my ollave,
little profit was it to anyone who should utter it—
he would not endure a breath against me.

From childhood he would share with me
(God reward O'Huiginn therefor)
every eager design that he formed
until it was time for us to part.

The teaching that I give today
to his pupils after the poet's death,
it was Ferghal Ruadh who made it:
O Lord that it were like his!

Dear is the mystic hut of poesy,
which I recognize after his loss:
O empty hut before me
thou wast not wont to have a neighbour.

That Aine's son lives not
has robbed poesy of her gaiety:
as a plank goes out of the side of a cask
the wall of learning has broken.

OSBORN BERGIN

A Court Poet in Trouble

A house where white hands are longer,
a house where white-soled feet are more slender,
a house where clustering locks were more brilliant,
and where hand-linen was more lustrous;

A house where shoulders and bosoms were whiter,
and where ladies were more red-lipped,
where locks were more curving-bright and yellow,
and blue eyes shaded by darker lashes;

A house wherein were more golden jewels,
a house wherein were more serving-men,
a house wherein were more dispensers of noble birth—
that has not been built and will not be built!

O Richard of Beann Bladhma,
forsake not the men of art.
Whatever exploit one may do
no one is famous without generosity.

OSBORN BERGIN

Abusive Snatches

I

I should not wonder
if Crundmail's tumble-down house
used salt for butter,
their skins are as shrivelled
as the bark of a dried-up tree.

II

No names—
but there's a certain woman:
her wind is like a stone
from a catapult.

III

Thou snatch of a man,
image of Satan,
comb in a pantry,
lascivious blue-bottle,
outworn, nether millstone,
useless fence to a yew-wood,
thou thirstless toper,
thou dirty-coloured shirt!

IV

Domungoirt!
lump of a skewered gosling,
blue-black gem of a devilish,
bloodless, reaving, beggarly
tongue of a one-eyed nun!

Thou greedy, wanton bull-calf,
bugling on a midden!
Thou bow-legged bug!
Thou swollen belly of a sick child . . .
Little use hast thou been to learning!

The Cad

O woman in the pantry,
unless you feed me good and plenty,
unless you let me gather
bread and butter from the larder,
I'll squeeze you in a corner,
and when I've ruined your honour,
I'll go and tell my master!

S. O'F.

Eulogistic Snatches

I

When you reach the top of Aigle,
the islands of Mod seem many.
The feet of all the flies of the world are many,
the treasures of Eilge are many,
the stars of the sky are many,
the waves of the sea are many.
But the guests of O'Donnell are far more numerous than
    any!

II

Mall Feball deserves reward.
He is dear to us,
our most beautiful, young king.
His hand is bright on the rim of the drinking-horn,
and see how hair hangs fair over his white shoulders.

III

Winter hurts me not,
hardship troubles me not,
even though the stags bellow on Druim No.
The king of Carrig Bla has received me—
my shafts of verse have struck their mark.

IV

Daughter of the brightest
of Leinster heroes!
Alike is the glitter
of her bracelets and her hair.

V

These goblets of the son of Donnacha
merit thanks—yellow antler-pledges.
We Frankish soldiers are a greedy lot:
we have been thirsty for their old mead.

KUNO MEYER

In Praise of a Harp

O harp of Cnoc I Cosgair:
that bringest sleep to eyes long wakeful,
thou of the sweet and delicate moan,
pleasant, refreshing, grave.

O choice instrument of the smooth, gentle curve,
thou that criest under red fingers,
musician that hast enchanted us,
red harp, high-souled, perfect in melody.

Thou that lurest the bird from the flock,
that coolest the heart,
brown, sweet-speaking, speckled one,
fervent, wondrous, passionate.

Thou healer of every wounded warrior,
charm that beguilest women,
familiar guide over the dark water,
music, mystic and sweet.

Thou silencer of all instruments of music,
shining, tuneful instrument,
thou dweller among the Children of Conn,
thou stout, dark-yellow tree.

Thou favourite of the learned,
restless, smooth one, sweetly musical,
red star over elf-mounds,
breast jewel of the high kings.

O sweet and gentle flowers!
O brown harp of Diarmuid!
O shape dear to every company,
thou voice of the cuckoos in May!

I have heard of no music like thy structure,
after the Tuatha De Danann,
O branch, dark and fine,
lovely fair . . . glorious.

O sound of the beach against the gentle wave,
shadowy tree of true melody,
feasts are consumed beside thee,
O voice of the swan on bright streams.

O cry of fairy women from the mound of Lir,
no music can match thine,
under thy guidance every house is sweet-stringed,
thou pinnacle of harp-music.

O'Connor of Conn's city!
grandson of O'Melaghlin,
happy men envy thy house,
thy castle is a weir of harps.

Osborn Bergin

Finis

Finis to all the manuscripts I've penned
and to life's fitful fever, here *The End;*
The End to lime-white women, golden-tressed—
and in God's hand at judgment be the rest.

ROBIN FLOWER

Notes and Index
of First Lines

Notes

A branch of Evin's apple tree: title-page:
> These are the opening lines of a long poem, for which see *The Voyage of Bran*. Edited by Kuno Meyer. London, 1895.

Starry Sky: page 29:
> Text (and literal translation) in *Zeitschrift für celtische Philologie*, 1 (1897), p. 327. Edited by Kuno Meyer.

The Vision of Ita: page 30:
> Text and translation in *The Martyrology of Oengus*. Edited by Whitley Stokes. London, 1905, p. 44. The vision here mentioned was vouchsafed to Ita for her patience in doing penance: see under January 15th: She kept "a stag-beetle as big as a lap-dog a-sucking her" until it "destroyed the whole of one of her sides." Robin Flower has written delicately of this legend in *Hymenaea and Other Poems*, p. 41. London, 1918: beginning:

He came to me
A little before morning through the night
And lay between my breasts until daylight.

How helplessly
Lay the small limbs, the fallen head of gold,
The little hands that clasped and could not hold.

And ending:

And thence he drew
With soft stirred lips and clutching hands that strove,
Sweet mortal milk of more than mortal love.

When morning grew
Far in the East and the world woke from rest
The King of Stars was quiet on my breast.

Ita is pronounced, in modern Irish, *Eeta*.

The Heavenly Banquet: page 31:
    Text and translation in *Materials for Ancient Irish History*.
Edited by Eugene O'Curry, p. 616. Dublin, 1861.
    I have transposed the last verse from its position at the
opening of the poem, and omitted one quatrain.
    This is the only poem of its kind that I have found in
connexion with the Irish Church, and it warms my heart
to think that we once had so much cheerful humanity
among our holy people.

Penitentes: page 32:
    Text and (literal) translations in *The Martyrology of Done-
gal*, pp. 281, 318, 326, 130, respectively. Edited by J. H. Todd
and W. Reeves. Dublin, 1864.
    If my facetious versions displease anyone, I can only say
I did them in that mood, deliberately.

The Desire for Hermitage: page 34:
    Text and editor's translation in *Eriu*, Vol. II, Part I, p. 55.
Edited by Kuno Meyer.
    There are fifteen quatrains in the original.

At Saint Patrick's Purgatory: page 35:
    These verses are from "a Maynooth manuscript" and were
printed without signature in the *Gaelic Journal*, IV, 190.
They are attributed to Donnchadh mor O'Dala, *m.* 1244:
"the greatest religious poet that Ireland has produced"—
Eleanor Hull, in *Textbook of Irish Literature*, I, 216. Dublin,
1910.

The Open-Air Scriptorium: page 39:
    Verses in the St. Gall Priscian: *Thesaurus Palæohibernicus*,

II, 290. Meyer ascribes the verses to the first half of the ninth century. The translation by Robin Flower may be found conveniently in *A Golden Treasury of Irish Verse*, p. 18. Edited by Lennox Robinson. London, 1925.

The Monk and His Cat: page 40:

Text in *Thes. Pal.*, II, 293. Meyer considered that the language is "late eighth or early ninth century." (*Ancient Irish Poetry*, p. 114.)

Pronounce Pangur Ban—*Pangur Bawn*.

In general it is to be noted that the vowels are more "open," or "back," than in English. *Pangur* is, thus, more like *Pongur*. *Sliabh* (the *h* aspirating the *b* into a *v*) is more like *shlee-ov* than *shlee-av*. The appearance of an *h* after a consonant always aspirates that consonant, sometimes virtually eliding it, as in Conchubhar, pronounced *Conahoor*. But both spelling and pronunciation are unpredictable, and it must always be a question as to how the ninth-century Irishman read these poems.

May Day: page 42:

Text in *Four Old-Irish Songs of Summer and Winter*, pp. 8 ff. Edited by Kuno Meyer. London, 1930. Translation in *Ancient Irish Poetry*, p. 54. In the latter book, p. 112, he says: "The date is the ninth century, I think." Mr. T. W. Rolleston's metrical translation of nine verses of this poem is in *An Anthology of Irish Verse*, p. 112. Edited by Padraic Colum. New York, 1922; and in *The High Deeds of Finn*. Harrap, London.

Summer Has Come: page 44:

Text in *Four Old-Irish Songs of Summer and Winter*, p. 20. Edited by Kuno Meyer. London, 1903. Taken from Selections from *Ancient Irish Poetry*, translated by Kuno Meyer, published by E. P. Dutton & Co., Inc., New York. Meyer says that "the piece probably dates from the tenth century."

Cuan Caill: pronounce *Cooan K(u)weel;* but, without

using technical phonetic symbols, it is impossible to reproduce the guttural, "open" quality of the diphthong in *Caill,* which is kept high up at the back of the palate.

Autumn Song: page 46:
Text and translation in *Eriu,* Vol. vii, Part i, p. 2. Edited by Kuno Meyer.

The verse translation is from *Dramatic Legends and Other Poems* by Padraic Colum, by permission of the Macmillan Company.

Cellach's Poem to the Dawn: page 47:
Text in *Silva Gadelica,* i, 56; ii, 59. Edited by Standish H. O'Grady. London, 1892. See Meyer's emendations of the text in *Revue Celtique,* xiv, 328. Dr. R. Flower has suggested a further change in l. 12, viz., *a chaindel.*

Pronounce Cluain Eo—*Clooyin Yeo.*

The Hermit and the King: page 50:
Text and translation in *King and Hermit.* Edited by Kuno Meyer, published by David Nutt, London, 1901.

Pronounce Marbhan—*Marwawn;* Roigne—*Royineh;* Maonmag—*Mwayon-maw;* Samhain—*Sow-in.*

Summer Is Gone: page 55:
Text in *Four Old-Irish Songs of Summer and Winter.* Edited by Kuno Meyer. London, 1903.

A Cold Night: page 56:
Text and translation in *Four Old-Irish Songs of Summer and Winter,* p. 18. Edited by Kuno Meyer. London, 1903.

The prose introductory paragraph is typical of a common habit among Irish scribes, who, affected by traditional regard for the "need" for such explanations, affixed to lyrics this kind of matter, mainly of their own invention. It is a scholastic trick, an effort, here, to swallow back the individual lyrists into the ossified traditions of the schools.

The same process is illustrated by the poem *Recollections of Caoilte*, p. 90.

The Song of the Sea: page 57:
Text (and translation) in *Otia Merseiana* (the publication of the Arts Faculty of the University of Liverpool), II, 76. Edited by Kuno Meyer. He dated the verses as eleventh century.
Pronounce Sliabh—*Slee-av*, or nearer to *Shlee-ov*.

The Blackbird's Nest: page 59:
This version is in *Irisleabhar na Gaedhilge* (The Gaelic Journal), IV, 42. Edited by Kuno Meyer. The verse translation is from *Bards of the Gael and Gall*, p. 180. Scribner's, London, 1897.

Wood to Burn and Not to Burn: page 61:
Text and translation in *Silva Gadelica*, I, 245; II, 278. Edited by Standish H. O'Grady.
Pronounce Iubhdan—*Yewdawn*.

Sea Snatches: page 64:
Text and German translation in *Abhandlungen der Akademie der Wissenschaften zu Berlin, Philos.-histor. Klasse,* 1919, no. 7, pp. 60–8, for I and II.
For III, text in University of Illinois: *Studies in Language and Literature,* Vol. II, Part 4, p. 42, 1916. Edited by Kuno Meyer.
For IV (*Storm in the Levant*), text in *Catalogue of Irish MSS. in the British Museum,* Vol. I, p. 336. London, 1926. Edited by Standish H. O'Grady. They are two quatrains of a longer but defective poem, conceivably written by an outward-bound pilgrim to the Holy Land.
For V (*The Scribe Revelling in the Safety of the Storm*), text in *Thes. Pal.,* II, p. 290. The literal translation may be found in *Ancient Irish Poetry*, p. 101. London, 1911. Edited by Kuno Meyer.

For VI (*The Corpse*), text in *Irische Texte*, Serie 4, Heft
1, p. 194. Edited by W. Stokes and E. Windisch. Leipzig,
1900.
Cascorach: pronounce *Cosscŏhroch;* the *ŏh* being held.

The Drowning of Conaing: page 66:

Text in *Irish Historical Grammar,* by Julius Pokorny,
Halle, p. 4. 1923. "The gods": Dr. Pokorny considers the
Bile Torten (mentioned in the original) to be Conaing's
tutelary tree, and Mr. Best in *Eriu,* Vol. IV, Part 2, p. 169,
places the Bili Tortan in Tortu, near Ardbraccan, County
Meath. Dr. Pokorny dates the verses as early eighth century.

The Three Most Famous Tales: page 69:

Text and (literal) translation in *Transactions of the Gaelic
Society in Dublin,* Vol. I, Pt. III, p. 13, 1808. The source is
not given and I do not know if the lines occur elsewhere in
print and do not know where O'Flanagan got them.

Pronounce Fiacra—*Feeŏchra;* Fionnuala—*Fionnooala;*
Aodh does not sound the *d;* Naoisi—*Naoisshe;* Ainnle—
(with an open, "back" *a*) as, also, Ardan, as if it were in
assonance with *organ.*

The Icebound Swans: page 70:

Text and translation in *Oidhe Cloinne Lir* (Soc. for the
Preservation of the Irish Language), Dublin, p. 28. 1883.
The translation here given is based on *Atlantis,* IV, 144.
Edited by Eugene O'Curry. London, 1836.

Deirdre Looks Back at Scotland: page 71:

Irische Texte, Serie II, Heft 2, pp. 127, 158. Edited by
Stokes and Windisch, Leipzig, 1887.

Pronounce Dun Fidga—*Doon Feeya;* Inis Draigen—
Innish Draiyen; Glen Laid—probably, *Glen Lway,* or *Lay;*
Glen Eitchi—*Glen Ettkheh;* Glen Da Ruadh—*Glen Daw
Rooah;* Draigen, again—*Draiyen.*

Deirdre's Lament over Naoisi: page 73:

Text in *Irische Texte,* Serie II, Heft 2, 145, trans. 172. Edited by Stokes and Windisch. Leipzig, 1887.

Pronounce Dun Monaid—probably *Doon Monna;* Cathbad—*Coffah;* Scathach—*Scohagh;* Boghmhain—*Bohvin.*

Deirdre and Conchobar: page 75:

Text in *Irische Texte,* I, 77 ff., where there are two poems from the second of which I have taken but the final quatrain and the first of which I have shortened considerably. Translation in *Atlantis,* III, 408–16. London, 1862. By Eugene O'Curry. The text I have printed is from LL, whereas O'Curry chose YBL; nevertheless his translation, which is in parts as tentative as any translation of either text must be, may be used to equal advantage with either text, since their differences are, for the most part, matters of spelling.

Emain is sometimes pronounced *Eevin;* sometimes *Owin.* I do not know which Deirdre would have said; if either. Conchobar is modern Connor; is sometimes pronounced, today, *Crohoor,* to "translate" Christopher. Probably Deirdre said *Cona(c)hooir.*

The Sleep-Song for Diarmuid: page 77:

Text (and editor's translation) in *Duanaire Finn.* Edited by E. McNeill. London, 1908. Vol. VII of the Irish Texts Society publications, pp. 84, 197.

Pronounce O'Duibhne—*O'Dw(u)eeneh;* Finncha—*Finnkheh;* Slaine—*Slawineh;* Binn—*Beeng;* Loch Carman—*Cor'mon;* Aine—*Awinneh,* or *Awine.*

Lament for Cael: page 80:

Text in *Irische Texte,* Serie 4, Heft 1, p. 24. Edited by Stokes and Windisch. Leipzig, 1884. Translation in *Silva Gadelica.* Vol. II, p. 122. Edited by Standish H. O'Grady.

Pronounce Rinn-da-bharc—*Reen-daw-vorc;* Druim-da-thren—*Druim-daw-hrain;* Druim Sileann—*Sheelan;* Tulach-leis—*Lesh;* Crimhthann—*Criffen.*

Conall's Head: page 82:
> Text: *The Book of the Dean of Lismore,* p. 73, Gaelic version. Edited by Rev. Thomas M'Laughlan. Edinburgh, 1862. Translated: *Bards of the Gael and Gall,* p. 176. Edited by George Sigerson. New York, 1907.
> No source is listed in the Dean's Book.
> Pronounce Ochagon—*Uch ochone.*

Cuchulainn's Lament for Ferdiad: page 86:
> Text and German translation in *"Die Altirische Heldensage Táin Bó Cúalnge," Irische Texte,* p. 597. Extra Band. Edited by E. Windisch. Leipzig, 1905. English translation in *Bards of the Gael and Gall,* p. 119, by George Sigerson. New York, 1907.
> Pronounce Ferdiad—*Ferdia.*

Fand Yields Cuchulainn to Emer: page 86:
> Text in *Irische Texte,* Serie 1, p. 224. Edited by E. Windisch. Leipzig, 1880. There is an English translation by Eugene O'Curry in *Atlantis,* ii, p. 119. London, 1859.
> Pronounce Cuchulainn—*Coohullin.*

The Fairy Midir's Invitation to Etain: page 87:
> Text in *Irische Texte,* i, 132. Edited by Ernst Windisch. Leipzig, 1880. Translation based on that by O'Curry in *Irish Manners and Customs,* iii, p. 191. London, 1873.
> Pronounce Inish Fail—*Innish Fawil.*

Recollections of Oisin: page 88:
> Text, and editor's translation, in *Duanaire Finn* (Irish Texts Society), Vol. vii, pp. 15, 112; edited by Eoin MacNeill. London, 1908.

Recollections of Caoilte: page 90:
> Text in *Irische Texte,* Serie 4, Heft 1, p. 100. Edited by W. Stokes and E. Windisch. Leipzig, 1900. Translation in *Silva Gadelica,* ii, 192, Standish H. O'Grady.

The introductory note was in all probability written by the scribe, not the poet. See note to *A Cold Night*.

The Blackbird of Derrycairn: page 92:
Text in *Eigse Suadh is Seanchaidh*, p. 51. Edited by the Irish Society of Maynooth. Dublin, 1908.
Mac Calpurn is Saint Patrick.
Pronounce Mac Cumhall—*MacCool;* Gleann-na-bFuath —*Glownavooah;* Cnoc-na-Scoth—*Knocknascoh;* Cnoc-na-Sealg—*Knocknashealg.*

Eve's Lament: page 94:
Text in *Eriu*, Vol. III, Part 2, p. 148. Edited by Kuno Meyer. He dated it as "probably late tenth or early eleventh century." The manuscript of the poem was compiled in 1628 by Michael O'Clery. There is a verse translation in *Lyrical Poems,* by Thomas MacDonagh, Dublin, 1913, p. 43.

Love Epigram: page 95:
Text in *Abhandlungen der Akademie der Wissenschaften zu Berlin*, p. 69, Nr. vii, 1919. *Bruchstücke der älteren Lyrik Irlands*. Edited by Kuno Meyer.
The final *d* of Muad is not heard, or only as an aspirate —*th.*

Liadain and Cuirithir: page 96:
Text in *Liadain and Cuirithir,* pp. 22 ff. Kuno Meyer, London, 1902. This famous ninth-century romance is preserved only in a fragmentary condition but it appears that the lovers submitted themselves to the guidance of a Saint for their soul's welfare and having loved passionately, but for one night only, entered religion as a nun and monk and parted for ever. The verse-translation by Mr. Frank O'Connor appeared in the *Dial* (New York) in April 1929. The poem is the subject of one of the earlier stories in George Moore's *A Story-Teller's Holiday*. London, 1918.

The Tryst with Death: page 98:
Text in *Fianaideacht,* Royal Irish Academy Todd Lecture Series, Vol. XVI, p. 10. Edited by Kuno Meyer. Dublin, 1910. I have shortened the poem considerably by omitting thirty-three quatrains, many of which are occupied with a description of the spoils. In *Ancient Irish Poetry,* p. 111. London, 1911. Meyer dated the verses ninth century.

Pronounce Féic—*Fayk;* Clarach—*Clawrakh;* Nia Nar—*Neea Nawr* (probably).

The Hag of Beare: page 101:
Text and translation in *Otia Merseiana,* I, 119. Ed. Kuno Meyer. The translation given is based on Meyer but he was not sure of some of the verses and in his translation in *Ancient Irish Poetry* (New York, 1911) he omitted several. Most of the emendations in the translation have been suggested to me by Mr. Patrick O'Donnell, M.A., but I should, however, acknowledge full responsibility. "On the mythical personage of the Caillech Berri I refer the student to my notes in the *Vision of MacConglinne,* pp. 131–4, 208–10. Stories are still told of her in Ireland and as Whitley Stokes points out to me a proverb is ascribed to her in Scotland" (Meyer). For three folk-tales connected with the Caillech Berri see Douglas Hyde's *An Sgealuidhe Gaedhealach,* pp. 284, 448, 520 (London, 1901). See also: "Legends and Traditions of the Cailleach Bheara": Eleanor Hull in *Folk-lore,* XXXVIII, no. 3, p. 225. Meyer considered that the verses here printed were of the tenth century—*Ancient Irish Poetry,* p. 113. The verses are frequently compared with Villon's *Regrets de la Belle Heaulmière ja parvenue à vieillesse.* Some may also be reminded of Horace, Ode XXV, Book I, on Lydia—*Parcius iunctas quatiunt fenestras.*

Pronounce Mugh—*Moo.* Beare is the modern, anglicized form (as in Bere Island) of Beara—*Bay'reh.*

Sweeney the Mad: page 106:

Text and translation in *The Adventures of Suibhne Geilt.*
Edited and translated by J. G. O'Keeffe. Irish Texts Society,
Vol. xii, pp. 28 ff.; 52 ff.; 62 ff. London, 1913.

I am very doubtful about the propriety of including this
long excerpt in a collection like this; the whole thing is
more like fiction than poetry, but as will be seen, poetry is
so dramatic in this Ireland that it is hard to say where lyric
ends and something else, that is not lyric, begins. I include
it for its extraordinary imaginative suggestiveness and its
human quality.

Suibhne becomes our Sweeney; here it is pronounced
(approximately) *Soo'eeneh;* Sliabh Mis—*Shleeov Mish;*
Glenn Aighle—*Ai'yleh;* Cuialgne—the *g* is not heard;
Eibhlinne—*Ei'linne* unless they said *Eivlinne,* the *b* being
either a *v,* or elided altogether; Fiodh Gaibhle—*Feeo'
Gaiyleh;* Dun Sobairce—*Doon Sovairķeh.*

Aran: page 119:

Text in *Irische Texte,* Serie 4, Heft 1, p. 10. Edited by Stokes
and Windisch. This is not the Irish but the Scottish *Aran.*
Like a great number of similar poems it is ascribed to Saint
Columcille.

Mananaan to Bran: page 120:

Text in *The Voyage of Bran,* i, 17. Edited by Kuno Meyer.
London, 1895.

On the Breaking-Up of a School: page 125:

Text and translation in *Studies,* Vol. xiii, p. 85. Edited by
Osborn Bergin.

A Court Poet in Trouble: page 128:

Text and translation in *Studies,* Vol. xiii, pp. 244, 246.
Edited by Osborn Bergin.

The *d* of *Bladhma* is not heard.

Abusive Snatches: page 129:
    Text and translation in *Abhandlungen der Akademie der Wissenschaften zu Berlin*, Nr. 7, pp. 33, 34, 27 (*bis*), respectively. Edited by Kuno Meyer.

The Cad: page 131:
    Text (and literal translation) in University of Illinois, *Studies in Language and Literature*, Vol. II, Part 4, p. 44. Edited by Kuno Meyer. 1916.

Eulogistic Snatches: page 132:
    Text and translation in *Abhandlungen der Akademie der Wissenschaften zu Berlin*, Nr. 7. 1919. Edited by Kuno Meyer. *Bruchstücke der älteren Lyrik Irlands.*

In Praise of a Harp: page 134:
    Text and trans. in *Studies*, Vol. XII, pp. 273, 276. Edited by Osborn Bergin.

Finis: page 136:
    From *Burduin Beaga*, p. 202. Edited by T. F. O'Rahilly, Dublin, 1925. Translation by Robin Flower in *Love's Bitter Sweet*, Cuala Press, Dublin, 1925.

Index of First Lines

[151]